Christian Healing
Rediscovered

Christian Healing Rediscovered

Roy Lawrence

KINGSWAY PUBLICATIONS
EASTBOURNE

© Roy Lawrence 1976

First published 1976
Reprinted 1979

ISBN 0 902088 93 9

Printed in Great Britain for
KINGSWAY PUBLICATIONS LTD.,
*Lottbridge Drove, Eastbourne, East Sussex BN23 6NT by
Hunt Barnard Printing Ltd., Aylesbury, Bucks.*

CONTENTS

PREFACE

Thank You

Many people have had a hand in the making of this book in one way or another. I do want to record my thanks to some of them – to the Principal and staff of Wycliff Hall, Oxford, who helped me to order my thoughts about Christian healing during a refresher course there; to the Clergy, Church officers and people of St George's Hyde who embarked so readily upon the investigation of the practicalities of Christian healing when I returned from Oxford to my parish; to the editorial staff of Christian Weekly Newspapers who invited me to write five articles on our experiences of healing; to Dr Jack Hywel-Davies, Managing Director of Coverdale House Publishers, who read one of these articles and asked me to expand them into a full book; to Pat Bradshaw who as an act of Christian stewardship served as my secretary at St George's, Hyde and typed the manuscript of this book; to the Reverend George Bennett who was such a guide and friend in the developing ministry of healing at St George's and who was kind enough to read and approve the manuscript of this book; to my wife Eira who not only patiently bore the preoccupied neglect which writers tend to heap upon their marriage-partners but also made many helpful comments out of her experience as a physiotherapist; to the churches, groups, and individuals who readily submitted to my investigations when I was compiling the appendices to this book and above all to the Lord and Giver of life and wholeness who calls today's Church and today's world to the rediscovery of healing and to whose call the story which now begins is a small act of response.

Roy Lawrence.

CHAPTER ONE

Making a Start

He could not move without pain.

I was a junior-student at the time. He was a church warden at a mission church where I was occasionally invited to assist at services. I had come to regard him with considerable respect. He had resigned from the firm for which he worked, on a point of principle, because he believed the company to be guilty of serious malpractice. He knew he was taking a risk and that there was a chance that his name would be blackened and that it would be hard for him to find other work, but he felt that as a Christian he had to make a stand.

To be without a job and without a reference was not easy, but there was worse to come. Soon after his resignation he became ill. The cause was difficult to trace but he was told by his doctor that it might be some sort of virus infection. He was housebound. Pains in his back and limbs kept him in continuous discomfort. The condition did not respond to treatment. For month after month there was no improvement. His wife became increasingly worried. His own spirit sank lower and lower.

Then one day when I was visiting him he said to me, 'You know, if Jesus was here, he'd shift all this. He'd heal me.' We thought about this in silence for a while and then it struck us both together, *Jesus was there*. We had his word for it. 'Where two or three are gathered together in my name, there am I' – and we two were gathered in his name. We soon knew what we had to do.

The next day we both spent the morning in prayer, I in the parish church and he at his home. In the afternoon I laid hands on him in the name of Christ. He started to improve almost immediately. A fortnight later he was riding his bicycle around the parish!

All this happened over twenty years ago and was my first conscious experience of Christian Healing.

Oddly enough, I then went on virtually to forget about it! It had been wonderful while it happened, but afterwards I found myself thinking – perhaps he would have got better at that time anyway, or perhaps it had all been psychosomatic. In any case I was just about to start studying for a degree in theology at Oxford and this sort of experience seemed strangely out of place in the cool detachment of academic study. So I tucked it away at the back of my mind.

*

Many years later I was one of a car-load of clergy on the way to a conference in Blackpool, and quite suddenly and casually someone said, 'Have you noticed that when Jesus says, "preach" he usually adds, "and heal"?'

It was just a chance comment but it was enough to bring the whole subject of Christian healing back into the forefront of my thoughts and I found that I could not forget it. It was a disturbing comment, because if Jesus has given his Church two equally important commands, 'preach and heal', then the Church has become lopsided. We preach our heads off – after a fashion – but the study and practice of healing has largely been lost over the centuries.

I was due to go back to Oxford for a half-term's refresher course and decided to spend part of the time looking at what the Bible has to say about healing. There I rediscovered certain basic truths which tend to be forgotten.

Healing is a primary biblical topic. In fact it is no exaggeration to say that *the Bible is a book about healing*. Its concern is the healing of the total man, body, mind and spirit, the healing of relationships, the healing of society, the healing of the nations.

'Bless the Lord, O my soul,' says the psalmist, 'and forget not all his benefits; who forgiveth all thine iniquities, who *healeth all thy diseases*' (Psalm 103: 2, 3). God's essential nature is that of a healer. One of his titles is 'The Lord who heals' (Exodus 15: 26). The biblical philosophy of life if accepted increases health. The book of Proverbs puts it quaintly but concisely, 'Fear the Lord, and depart from evil: it shall be health to thy navel and marrow to thy bones' (Proverbs 3: 7, 8).

It followed that since Jesus came into the world to do the will of God (John 6: 38), healing was the will and the work of Jesus. He 'came forth and saw a great multitude, and he had compassion on them and healed their sick' (Matthew 14: 14). Along with the mass healings there were many instances of individual healings – blindness (Matthew 9: 27–31), deafness (Mark 7: 31–35), lameness (Matthew 11: 4, 5), paralysis (Matthew 8: 5–13), fever (Matthew 8: 14, 15), skin conditions (Matthew 8: 1–3), and so on.

Also, Jesus made it plain that it was his will to continue his healing ministry through his Church. My colleague in the car on the way to Blackpool was right. Christ's dual commission was 'preach *and heal*' (Luke 9: 1, 2 and 6; Luke 10: 1 and 9). The early disciples were obedient and effective in the ministry of healing. There were mass healings (e.g. Acts 5: 16) and individual healings (Acts 3: 1–16; 9: 32–43; 14: 8–10; 28: 8, 9).

Jesus saw healing as a sign and an element in the coming of the Kingdom of God (Luke 10: 9). Isaiah had seen it in the same way centuries earlier (Isaiah 35: 4–6).

James spelt out the practicalities for a Christian congregation. 'Is any among you sick? Let him call for the elders of the Church; and let them pray over him, anointing him with oil in the name of the Lord; and the prayer of faith shall save him that is sick, and the Lord shall raise him up; and if he have committed sins, it shall be forgiven him. Confess therefore your sins, one to another, and pray one for another, *that you may be healed*' (James 5: 14–16).

But what of ourselves? Most clergy, I would guess, could tell of isolated incidents in which they have prayed with the sick and perhaps laid on hands in the name of Christ and there have been remarkable occasions of healing.

As I thought of it for myself, the incident of the healing of the church warden came back into my mind and I remembered that after my ordination there were other similar incidents, not all that many, perhaps one every couple of years. Other clergy with whom I talked described much the same situation. Christian healing was an actuality for us – but an occasional one. It tended to be on the periphery of our thought and practice. We tended to think of it as an extra, and a rather surprising one.

This clearly is not good enough. It is not the sort of balance which Jesus had in mind when he envisaged the ministry of his disciples. 'Preach and heal' does not mean two sermons every Sunday and a healing perhaps every other year! He did not lead us to expect a diminution in the availability of healing power. The disciples were to do more, not less, than Jesus did (John 14: 12)! Was he perhaps just thinking of the spread of the message of salvation when he told them this? Was he excluding the ministry of healing? Not at all. For salvation and healing are inseparably interrelated in the Bible. In fact in our English New Testament 'save' and 'heal' often translate the same Greek word. 'Sozo' and 'diasozo' mean both 'save' (94 times in the New Testament) and 'heal' (16 times in the New Testament).

As my refresher course at Oxford went on its way, I could see all this with increasing clarity.

The question was – what was I going to do about it when the time came for me to return to my parish?

CHAPTER TWO

Towards a Service of Healing

There were various options open to me when I returned from the half-term refresher course at Oxford to my parish of St George's, Hyde. I could have said nothing to anybody but quietly intensified the element of healing in my personal pastoral ministry. This really did not seem sufficient. Or I could have gathered a like-minded group and started a small mid-week service of prayer for healing. This did not seem sufficient either. If healing is the basic life and work of the whole Church, it is not sufficient to tuck it away in a corner. I felt a strong leading to introduce the theme of Christian healing into the main stream of the worship of my church at a regular Sunday service.

There were difficulties of course. There was my ignorance, which was vast. There were my doubts which had to be acknowledged and faced. 'How do I know it really works? Suppose my experiences so far have all been coincidences?' There were my fears. 'Supposing it all goes wrong? What will be left of my faith? Will I look a fool? Is there a chance I might actually harm people by giving them false hope?'

But amid the mental turmoil there was at any rate one absolute certainty. I knew without doubt that Christian healing is a topic of such importance and such biblical centrality that it is vital for the Church to be looking at it hard and straight, researching into it, bringing thought, prayer, Bible-study, and the light of historical and personal experience to bear upon an honest serious investigation till we know both the facts of the matter and the nature of God's call to us.

Normally we do not do this – or so it seems to me. We take up what appears to be basically a hypocritical position. On the one hand we preach about the healing miracles as though they did happen. On the other hand we act as though they did not happen. We even pray as though they did not happen

13

– introducing the words 'if it be thy will' as a sort of safety-clause in prayer for healing. This type of 'double-think' is neither honest nor effective. If we know that Christian healing is a fundamentally important matter but we are not sure where faith and fact should be leading us, the honest thing is to say so and to start looking and learning.

So having talked it over with the Parochial Church Council, what we did was to start a monthly service of 'Investigation into Christian Healing'. It took place on the first Sunday of the month at 6.30 p.m. Basically it was the Anglican service of Evensong, but there were one or two differences. In the intercessions we prayed by name for sick folk known to us. At first the list was fairly short but quickly as the practice became known the list became longer. We used the same list of names for intercession week by week at a Thursday mid-morning Communion service, and the list was left hanging on the wall at the back of the church in the hope that people would come in and use it for private prayer.

The sermon at an 'Investigation into Christian Healing' was an examination of some aspect of healing. During the first year we looked in broad terms at the place of healing in the life and teaching of Jesus, at its place in the teaching of the Bible as a whole, at the actual historical experience of the Church, and at personal experiences, both my own and those shared with me by other people. We tried both to use our powers of reason and to be sensitive to the guiding of the Holy Spirit. From the second year onwards we began to go chapter by chapter through Luke's Gospel, paying particular attention to the theme of healing as it arose – and finding that it always did arise in one way or another. We bought copies of Luke's Gospel from the British and Foreign Bible Society. These were handed to members of the congregation as they entered church and collected before they left, so that all could have the text before them as the sermon was preached.

Following the sermon a laying on of hands in the name of Christ was made available to anyone wishing to receive it. Anyone was free to come to the communion rail during the singing of the hymn after the sermon. The invitation was always put in the widest terms, 'You are welcome to receive a laying on of hands and a prayer in the name of Christ if you wish to do so for any reason at all. Perhaps you have been ill in some way and have a need for physical healing. Perhaps you are feeling anxious or depressed or have a need for mental healing. Perhaps some temptation is hard to cope with and you are conscious of the need for spiritual healing. Or if you wish, you may come forward just as an act of commitment, a prayer for spiritual deepening. Or perhaps you want to come forward as an act of prayer for someone else, whom you know to be in need of healing. The touch of Christ is desirable for its own sake, quite apart from any by-products it may bring. So whatever your reasons for coming forward you are welcome.'

Two of us were behind the communion rail, a clergyman and a layman. First we administered a laying on of hands to each other with the prayer, 'May the healing power of the Holy Spirit be in you'. Then we waited for any who wished to come forward, ready to offer the same prayer and the same touch. Out of a congregation of about a hundred, thirty or forty came forward on the first occasion to kneel at the communion rail. The number was about the same at each of the healing services during the first eighteen months. As there were three clergy on the staff and a fair number of suitable laymen and women we were able to vary the ministrants month by month.

The words of the prayer, 'May the healing power of the Holy Spirit be in you', were said in unison by the two ministrants. The congregation stood for the singing of the hymn and then knelt in silence while the laying on of hands was completed. Month by month we studied and prayed and laid on hands and waited to see what would happen.

The first thing we noticed was that there was a steady and perceptible improvement in the quality of the worship. St George's, Hyde, is a 'chatty' church. Before and after services there is a buzz of conversation. It was so well entrenched as a habit, that short of sticking plaster over the congregation's lips as they entered I could see no way of stopping it! However before a service of healing the church was noticeably quieter – and sometimes even absolutely quiet. During the service there was often an atmosphere of extraordinary spiritual concentration. This had nothing to do with emotionalism. Our services of healing have always been unemotional, more akin to a Communion service than to an evangelistic rally. However, having said that, the second noticeable feature of these services was the opportunity which they presented for Christian challenge. Healing and the proclamation of the gospel got together naturally – and I would say inevitably. Christian healing is a ministry to the whole man. It cannot be divorced from the gentle exposition of the saving power of Christ.

The odd thing was that during the first eighteen months of our services of healing the one thing which we did not see was physical healing. We looked for it and longed for it – over-much as we later came to think – but we did not see it. In fact it seemed that there was more than our normal ration of sickness in the church during these eighteen months. The church officers and I also became increasingly aware of some of the problems and difficulties associated with Christian healing.

At this stage we took an important decision. We acknowledged our need for help. We knew enough of the problems and the issues. We needed the help and guidance of someone who not only knew the problems but also knew some of the answers and had tested these answers on the anvil of his own experience.

CHAPTER THREE

Help

We were fortunate in finding exactly the help we needed – it came to us through the ministry of George Bennett, a remarkable man with a remarkable mission.

George Bennett was ordained in the Church of England back in 1935. Brought up in a medical family he had begun to study medicine at Birmingham university when he experienced a conversion from agnosticism to Christianity and was called to the ministry. During the earlier part of his ministry he was in turn a curate, a vicar, a hospital chaplain, an industrial chaplain and a Cathedral canon. But his main work was to begin in 1958 when he took charge of a centre at Crowhurst in Sussex which devoted itself to Christian healing. This centre has come to be regarded with widespread respect. It has been visited by and registered with the Medical Officer of Health and listed in the King Edward's Hospital Directory and hundreds of patients have passed through and benefited from it. The story of this centre is told by George Bennett in his book 'Miracle at Crowhurst', which, along with the companion volume 'The Heart of Healing', has itself exercised a ministry of healing amongst readers.

For some years now George Bennett has made himself free to answer invitations to address groups, lead conferences and conduct missions here and overseas and has travelled to the far side of the world healing and teaching. I met him for the first time when B.B.C. Radio Manchester sent me to conduct a brief interview with him for a religious magazine programme. The producer and I were both very impressed with him on this occasion. Simplicity, balance and holiness shone through the interview. So it was arranged that on Sunday 24th June 1974 George Bennett would speak at our evening service, expounding the Church's healing role in society, on the Monday evening he would answer 'Any Questions', and on the Tuesday evening he would conduct a service of Christian healing. It was also arranged that the visit would include a half-hour broadcast on Radio Manchester and a day conference for clergy of the Diocese of Chester.

We had six months to prepare for the mission. We wrote to local clergy, doctors, nurses, physiotherapists, probation officers, social service workers, and others to tell them what was happening and, where necessary, to present the case for a spiritual dimension in healing. We also circularised a thousand homes. Two very encouraging things happened in the weeks immediately before the mission. Three local churches, two Anglican and one Free Church, cancelled their own evening services on Sunday 23rd June so that their clergy and congregations could participate fully in the mission. Other churches indicated their willingness to participate on the Monday and Tuesday evenings. This in a neighbourhood where traditionally there has been a certain competitiveness between the churches was itself a work of healing. Also for the first time since our healing services started there began to be reports of healing. Granada Television asked for permission to televise part of the healing service and after some hesitation while we said our prayers and thought about it, it seemed right to agree.

So the mission began, and very memorable it proved. It was memorable for the quality of worship. The singing was terrific. The atmosphere of prayer was strong and full of power, though, as in the case of our own 'Investigation into Healing' services there was no undue emotionalism. The mission was memorable for the cutting of denominational differences down to size. Since then there has been a marked improvement in interdenominational and interchurch relationships in Hyde. The mission was certainly a major factor in this. The mission was memorable also for the record number of questions on the Monday evening – exceeding every other place George had visited, including his American visits! It was memorable for the numbers attending – eight hundred on the Tuesday with over seven hundred receiving a laying on of hands from George Bennett and a team of six local clergy. The half hour programme on B.B.C. Radio Manchester was also memorable. Tape recordings of it have been used subsequently to stimulate many a church group. And the conference for clergy of the Diocese of Chester was a great occasion, making an impact on many a ministry.

The Tuesday evening was a night to remember. We knew the TV crew quite well by then. The producer, director and researcher attended church on all three nights, though the job itself did not require them to do so. We had some misgivings about their presence. The church was quite cluttered with extra lights and TV equipment. We knew that there would be people in church for whom the service would mean a great deal, people whose needs were great and whose hopes were great. It would have been very sad if they were to be distracted or if the service were to be turned into some sort of a show. We need not have worried. The TV crew said that they had never been so ignored in their life! We sang a selection of hymns. I led a prayer – extempore, though that is not my normal custom. George Bennett spoke briefly. Then the people came forward by the hundred to receive the laying on of hands in the name of Christ. Most did not receive the touch of George Bennett. He was flanked by three clergy on each side. So there were fourteen hands and only two were George's. But he made it quite clear that this was irrelevant, that it was not the touch of Bennett but the touch of Christ which heals and that the touch of Christ is conveyed by the Body of Christ, the Church.

Afterwards there was a TV interview at the Vicarage involving George Bennett and the TV interviewer Mike Scott. The TV crew stayed on for hours after their job was finished, talking, asking questions, drinking endless cups of coffee. The producer said that for the first time that evening he had seen what worship was actually for. He had seen the point of hymns, the point of prayer, the point of a Christian congregation. I missed most of it because in the middle of it all a man who was feeling suicidal turned up for counselling. But in due course he went home, and the TV people went away, and next day George Bennett went home. And it was over. Or was it?

CHAPTER FOUR

A Flow of Healing

It was almost as though arranging the Mission of Teaching and Healing turned on a tap. The healings started to flow – physical, mental and spiritual in their effect.

They started before the actual mission. For instance a man who had been off work for months with high blood-pressure found that following a laying on of hands his blood-pressure became absolutely normal. Beforehand, he had to take tablets to combat the high blood-pressure. Afterwards, not only did he no longer need the tablets, they actually made him feel ill. Without them he was normal. There was nothing to prove it had anything to do with Christian Healing. It could have been a coincidence. But if so, it was the first of many such 'coincidences'.

I was asked to see a housewife who was suffering from a phobic condition. She was in a sorry state, afraid to leave the house, afraid to answer the door, afraid even to answer the telephone. We talked for over an hour. We prayed together and I administered a laying on of hands in the name of Christ. Within minutes the condition began to lift. Next day she felt normal. She was able to go out into the town centre and do the family shopping without ill effect. The phobia did not return.

One of the congregation had a heart incident. Her doctor told her that she should give up smoking, but when I visited her she said that she was incapable of doing so. She said she was a slave to cigarettes. As she lay in bed, there was an open packet of cigarettes on the bedside table. She said she just had to have it there within easy reach. I said to her, 'Let's see what the Lord can do about it.' There and then we prayed together, not specifically about the cigarettes, but about the goodness and power and love of Christ. In his name I administered a laying on of hands. A fortnight later I met her leaning on her gate. 'You'll never believe it,' she said.

'I haven't had a single cigarette since you visited me. I just haven't wanted to.' Since then she has not smoked. The urge has gone.

With the mission came other reports of healing. For instance, the mother-in-law of a local fish and chip shop proprietor had suffered for ten years with swollen painful legs. She found it difficult to walk and had to be assisted into church at the mission service of healing. She was brought forward for a laying on of hands. The hands were not those of George Bennett, but belonged to a young clergyman who was feeling rather depressed and inadequate in the ministry. It was a characteristic gesture of God that this young clergyman's hands were used in the first instance of healing reported in connection with the mission. As the woman returned to her seat, she said to her son-in-law, 'All the pain has gone.' By the time she arrived back home her legs not only felt normal, they looked normal. Six months later I met her in the street and hardly recognised her. She looked ten years younger. Before, she could hardly walk. Now she could run! She could dance!

That particular family did rather well from the mission. The chip shop proprietor's wife had for some time suffered from back pains. She told me that tests had revealed a urinary infection. After the service of healing the back pains ceased and further tests showed that there was now nothing amiss.

A man with an acute depression wrote to me before the mission. He wondered whether he could find help because life was hardly worth living. A fortnight later he telephoned to say that his condition had improved remarkably. He had been able to stop all his tablets except for a couple of sleeping pills. He felt and sounded a new man.

I am well aware that as I write these words it is still too soon to assess these and many other reports with any sort of accuracy. However there was no mistaking the gladness and peace on the faces of dozens of people who talked with me about the personal meaning of the mission for them. They spoke of burdens being lifted, of new dimensions of living and of new glimpses of the reality and meaning of Christ. One pensioner said it was like starting life all over again!

I heard too of a healing over a year before – an unpleasant and recurrent skin condition which cleared completely after a period of counselling and laying on of hands. If only we

could have heard of this earlier. It happened in the middle
of the period when there seemed to be no signs of physical
healing anywhere and we were soldiering on with our services of 'Investigation into Christian Healing' in spite of an
apparent lack of results. It would have been such an encouragement to have known about it at the time.

However in a strange way, though we were now hearing of
these and other healings, they were less important to us than
they would have been before. For we were now learning more
clearly the difference between Christian healing and the mere
working of cures. Christian healing is concerned not so much
with cures as with wholeness; with that harmony with God
which helps a man to be more of a person than he was before,
spiritually, mentally, physically. Christian healing lifts up the
risen Christ not as a means to an end but as an end in itself.
We all need healing. We all need Christ. In a Christian healing service we seek the touch of Christ upon our lives, simply
because Christ is infinitely desirable. Cures, lovely though
they are, are just by-products.

Cures are not the only by-products of a venture in
Christian healing. The discernible deepening in the quality
of worship and the sharpened capacity for evangelism have
already been mentioned. They continued to develop. So too
did the increasing sense of Christian unity. For example a
local non-conformist church has decided that once a quarter
it will close its own evening service so that minister and
congregation can be one with the people of St George's in
our Service of Healing. This joint service is always a happy
and worthwhile occasion to which I look forward. It is good
also to receive letters of encouragement and support from
people of all denominations – a Baptist minister in Kent, a
doctor who has become a minister, a retired sea-captain, a
Cornish vicar, a Roman Catholic nun in a French Convent
who prays for the healing ministry of St George's, Hyde, on
the first Sunday of each month at 6.30 p.m. Everywhere it
seems there are new friends, new partners in healing.

We seem to have been given a sharpened awareness of the
basic issues of the Faith. It was, for instance, a real pleasure
to be at the meeting of the Parochial Church Council which
followed the mission. Member after member spoke of the
meaning which the mission had held for him personally.
Two members of the congregation have now offered themselves for the ministry – an event unheard of in the life of our

church before! And surprisingly we are finding that groups of the congregation are being invited to talk to other churches and other groups to share our experience of Christian healing and other discoveries which we are making about the meaning of being a responsible member of a responsible Church. We find that in God's economy nothing is wasted. We learned much during the first eighteen months investigating Christian healing and we are able to use it all now.

There is another by-product of our involvement in healing which should be mentioned. I hesitate to write about it because it was strange and painful and I would prefer to forget it. But it should be included both for the sake of completeness and in case others have to face it. Some weeks after the mission, even though we were surrounded by lovely and encouraging events, a number of our church leaders underwent a period of darkness and oppression. It happened simultaneously to all three clergy, to the Church Wardens and to the Church Secretary. It was a horrible thing, full of morbid fancies and the temptation to despair. Previously I had assumed that only the attractive could tempt, but it is not so. Strangely enough, my own experience of this oppression took place actually during a holiday period. All around me were scenes of beauty. There was opportunity for leisure and enjoyment. Yet through it all there was something horrid, hard to describe, a sort of weight of darkness, pressing down. It was a relief to find that others were going through it too. With mutual support and prayer it passed. It has been suggested to us that we were under some sort of attack – and certainly this is just what it felt like.

As we gathered our wits after this strange experience, we discovered a renewed sense of expectancy. I felt able to rename our service on the first Sunday of the month. Till then it had been an 'Investigation into Christian Healing'. Now we felt able to call it a 'Rediscovery of Christian Healing'. Our ignorance was still great. It *is* still great. But in one way and another our experience had led us to the point where we now knew that there is a deep reality of healing to be rediscovered if we are faithful to our Lord.

CHAPTER FIVE

Why did one man live and the other man die?

Perhaps this is the right point to look at a problem which is inevitably raised by an honest consideration of Christian healing, a problem to which so far I have found no completely satisfactory solution – the problem of the unhealed. Put in a nutshell the difficulty is this: if Christian healing sometimes works in a physical sense, why does it not always do so?

I can highlight this problem by telling two contrasting stories. In my last parish, one of my church wardens had to go into hospital for an operation. Something went wrong and instead of improving afterwards he became steadily worse. He could not eat. His weight loss was appalling. One of the doctors told me he had no chance of recovery. But he was wrong. We organised wide-spread prayer for him. I prayed with him in hospital and administered a laying on of hands. And against all the odds he started to eat again and to recover strength. His recovery was complete and he went on to serve as a vigorous church warden for a further ten years.

Contrast the story of a sidesman in my present parish – in many ways a closely similar story. He too underwent an operation. Afterwards his condition became markedly worse. He could not eat. There was an appalling weight loss. I was told he had no chance of recovery. He was expected to die early in 1972. Again wide-spread prayer was organised. I prayed with him and administered a laying on of hands. He started to eat and to recover strength. The spring, summer and autumn of 1972 passed and then quite suddenly in November he died. It was true that he had lived six bonus months, that the end was peaceful and that both he and his wife received extraordinary strength of spirit. She is still a strong, positive influence in the life of the church. But the fact remains that he died.

Why did one man live and the other die? There was no

lack of faith on the part of the sidesman and his wife. What then? I cannot believe those who suggest that sometimes God chooses to heal, sometimes not to heal. God never ceases to be 'the Lord who heals'. He does not change.

If I had to attempt an answer to the enigma, it would be something like this. There are laws governing the universe; laws of logic, laws of nature, laws of life. We are beginning to have a better understanding of some of them but there is much to learn. God does not break these laws. They are part of his own nature. When we pray for physical healing and it does not happen, some factor within the laws of life is preventing it. There would be no failure of healing in a perfect world, but this sinful world is far from perfect and contains many a block to healing. Very often we cannot see where the block lies. It may not be in the sufferer at all. For myself I am sure that it never lies in God.

This obviously does not constitute a complete or satisfactory answer, but the facts are that sometimes physical healing follows prayer and the laying on of hands, sometimes it does not. It does no honour to the Lord of truth to deny these facts or to produce explanations which are glib or superficial.

There are a few practical points which may be added. They do not answer the problem but they do help in actually coping with a situation of sickness. Perhaps also they help to indicate some of the blocks which can hinder healing.

1. *It is not helpful to long too much for purely physical healing. One can overpray at a physical level.* As a ministrant one can communicate more of one's own anxiety than of the calm strong love of Christ. As a patient one can actually resist the healing process by keeping one's attention on the need for it to take place. Insomnia provides a simple illustration. Longing to go to sleep, striving to go to sleep is no help at all. Praying to go to sleep may not be much better. But accept that sleeping or waking you can offer the night to God, relax in his presence, enjoy his acceptance, his peace, his love, his healing, know that you are in his arms, and the odds are that once you stop looking for sleep, it comes looking for you.

2. *Physical health, whilst it is a lovely God-willed thing, is not the whole or the deepest part of health.* At our mission of teaching and healing a young wife came forward for a laying on of hands. She was a keen Christian but bitter because she was suffering from multiple sclerosis. Afterwards

the multiple sclerosis seemed untouched but the bitterness had gone. It would be wrong to say that there was no healing.

3. *Christian healing does not actually focus the mind on ailments but on positive spiritual truth.* One of my congregation expressed some disquiet when he started with services of Healing. He was afraid they would turn us into hypochondriacs. I could see the point, but he had got it wrong. When we minister the laying on of hands in the name of Christ at a service, we do not put our minds on the troubles of the people who are kneeling at the communion rail, but we fill our minds with the picture of the risen Christ.

If you are ill it is good not to think too much about the ailment but to focus attention on a healing sequence of ideas and to go through them again and again. For instance each person of the Holy Trinity can provide a healing train of thought.

God the Father made me – he loves me – the creative energies of God are around me and in me. Jesus healed the sick – he is alive today – he has not changed – he still heals – and he is with me now. Come Holy Spirit – you are the giver of life and health – come into every part of me – let your healing power move in me, work in me, live in me – overflow from me, use me in the healing of the world.

In thought sequences such as these Christ will touch us and though we may be ill he will do us good. The illness may not be better – but *we* shall be better. Maybe both. But it is better not to dictate the form of healing he will bring.

4. *We shall not know the full possibilities of Healing by the power of Christ in the Church of Christ, till the Church as a whole takes Christian healing much more seriously.* I am sure that we and the world are suffering from lack of faith and lack of commitment on the part of the Church as a whole. If your left leg wanted to step forward but your right leg did not, you would do the splits rather than make progress. The Church is rather like that. It is a divided body, some members stepping forward, others dithering or falling back. We have the command of Christ – 'Heal'. What are we waiting for?

5. *In the meantime remember that God can bring good out of any situation, even sickness and death.* He can bring good out of it whether physical healing comes or not. 'All things work together for good for those who love God.' It is important to look for the blessing, the positive opportunity,

the golden thread in the worst situation – to look for it, thank God for it, and offer it trustingly in his service. It is surprising how much good can come out of bad times. The ultimate example must be Calvary. Nothing could have seemed worse. Physical pain, mental agony, spiritual dereliction – but God used it to redeem the world!

CHAPTER SIX

Why does a God of love allow suffering?

My last parish was full of children. It was said that elderly people kept off the streets for fear of being run down by prams! With so many children around sometimes one came across appalling tragedies. One of the worst was an occasion on which a young father ran over his baby in his drive. He had several children and when he was backing his car out of the garage he usually kept a close watch on them to see that they were not in the way. But one day he failed to see that his youngest child, still a baby, had crawled behind the car. He knew about this only when his rear wheels went over the baby's body. The father was in a terrible state afterwards, as was the mother. When I visited her, she lay in bed moaning over and over again, 'What did I do to deserve it? What sin did I commit? Why has God punished me like this?'

It is a question that recurs in one form or another throughout the life of a clergyman. I remember it being asked soon after I became a curate when I had to take the funeral of a young child who had died from cancer. I was asked it again a few days before I wrote this chapter. A woman sat in my study. Her husband whom she adored had died of a heart attack soon after retiring. 'Why did God take him?' she asked. 'What wrong had he done? He was a good man. He deserved better than this.' She was full of bitterness. She admitted she had been railing against God, blaspheming, cursing the God whom she believed was responsible. I tried to tell her, as I have tried to tell many others, that God did *not* do it. God is a God of life and health and joy, not of suffering, disease and tragic premature death. So where do these things come from, if not from the will of God?

There seem to be three types of suffering. First there is suffering which we bring upon ourselves. For instance, if I drink myself silly and next morning have a hangover I have only myself to blame. It is what the army calls 'a self-inflicted

28

wound'. Much venereal disease must come into the same category.

Secondly there is the suffering which we bring on each other. This is a most extensive category. It includes obvious instances like the drunken driver who knocks over a pedestrian and injures him. The injury is not the pedestrian's doing, but neither is it God's doing. It is a man-made situation caused by the interaction of one person with another. Again venereal disease is not only a 'self-inflicted wound'. One person infects another with it. Parents pass it to their children. In thinking of types of suffering which we bring on each other, we must also include those diseases for which we have a collective responsibility as members of society and of the human race. Many stress diseases, many road accidents, and diseases connected with the misuse and pollution of the world in which we live are of this sort. They are experienced individually but caused collectively. So are malnutrition diseases which are completely unnecessary in a world as rich in resources as ours. So are all the horrors associated with war.

The third category simply consists of types of suffering which seem not to come under the first two headings. It is interesting to note that this is a rapidly diminishing category. With increasing knowledge we are continually able to move individual types of disease or suffering from the third group to the first or second. For instance till recently no cause was known for lung cancer, but now we know that we can bring it on ourselves by smoking and bring it on each other by polluting the atmosphere.

It would seem that though we live in a universe where there is a certain amount of built-in risk, the greater part of disease and suffering is demonstrably man-made in one way or another. However if God does not cause it himself, there is still a problem. Why does he allow man to cause it?

Strangely the answer seems to be connected with God's *love*. If God is love, then it is to be expected that he will create and that he will wish to love his creatures. Man was created to be loved by God, to explore and enjoy and reflect that love. But in order to love and be loved he had to be free. You can't love a robot or a puppet. So man was given free will. Free will is the most wonderful gift in the world. God actually restricted his own freedom when he gave it – a miracle in itself. But it is also the most terrible gift in the world. If it is a genuine gift, we must be free to use it or misuse it. We can love and serve God or we can play at being our own god and reject love and replace it with selfishness, greed and hate. We can hurt ourselves and hurt each other. Free will is a dangerous thing, but if God were to take it away he would destroy us. We would no longer be people. So God leaves us our free will and we use it stupidly, sinfully, to bring suffering into the world. Sometimes we cause suffering just through ignorance, by accident. Freedom is a hazardous business. But if the risks are great, the positive potentialities are beyond conception. There is a risk of self-destruction but there is a potential for glory which defies description. This is particularly so when one sets the whole issue in the context of eternity as we shall seek to do later.

One further thing must be said in discussing the problem of suffering. If God allows suffering this does not mean that he acquiesces in it. Having given us free will God has not washed his hands of us. He is not just an interested bystander watching to see whether the human race will make the grade or whether we shall be our own unmaking. Without diminishing human free will, without manipulating us or coercing us in any way, God is a God of involvement, a God of healing. The creative energies of the Father are all around us and deep within us rich in healing power. Jesus is a living redemptive healing reality, freely available to all who will open themselves to him. The Holy Spirit, Lord of life and health, is the greatest gift of all time. It is for us to accept or reject the healing power of God, to co-operate with him or to resist him. The problem of suffering is not only an issue to be discussed, it is more than an academic problem, it is a battle-field, a call to action, a challenge to involvement, an opportunity for healing.

So far this chapter has been necessarily speculative, but it seems right to end it in a practical way. What can we say to any who at this moment are undergoing a time of personal tragedy or suffering and who feel confused or bitter about it? Who ask, 'Why should it happen to me?' Here are five thoughts which, I believe, have healing in them for people who feel this way.

1. It is useful to turn the question round and ask, 'Why should it *not* happen to me?' If we live in a world where for one reason or another suffering is a fact of life, why should it *not* happen to me? Why should suffering always be reserved

for the other fellow? Why should I be immune? What is so special about me? Certainly it would be nice to have an immunity badge, but Jesus never promised one to his followers. He promised not immunity but victory, which is a different thing.

2. If it is in your heart to rage against God, then rage away. God can do something with honest rage. He can do nothing with pretended piety. I sometimes recommend to my startled congregation the practice of 'swear prayers'. When the world seems intolerable and you feel sick and angry, say so honestly and in your own language. God knows you feel like that anyway, so why not say so? I said this to the woman who was in my study a few days ago, raging at the loss of her husband. Even though God did not himself will the premature death of her husband he will not back away from her rage. He will not answer rage with condemnation or rejection. So picture God in Christ hanging on the cross. Let your rage ram the crown of thorns on. Let your rage hammer in the nails. He will still love you.

3. Know that God understands – really understands. Part of the message of the Cross of Jesus is that God understands suffering from the inside. He suffers when we suffer. When I celebrate Holy Communion in the side chapel at St George's, Hyde, before me there is a cross which was given in 1920 by some parents who had lost their seventeen-year-old son. In the loss of their son they turned to the God who had lost his own son and in their minds they held the two events together. I hope they found healing in doing so.

4. Don't resist healing by over-cherishing bitterness. It is easy to clutch a grudge against the universe, to refuse to let it go, but it does no good. Be ready for healing when it comes whether it comes through time, or through the love of family and friends, or specifically through the love and power of Jesus.

5. When you have finally found a way of facing the situation and you can cope with life again, watch out for others who are still enmeshed by personal suffering or tragedy. In a unique way you will be able to help them out of the reserve of your own experience.

CHAPTER SEVEN

Medicine and Religion

In the last two chapters we have looked at two large problems – Why does Christian healing sometimes bring a physical cure and sometimes not? And why do suffering and disease exist at all if God is loving and good?

We turn now to a further problem – that of the relationship between Christian healing and medical science. Fortunately, unlike the other two, this really is hardly a problem at all – or so I reckon. I fail to see why logically there should be any sort of clash between Christian healing and medical science. One of my happiest experiences of healing involved close step by step co-operation with a local doctor as together we tried to bring healing to a teenaged girl suffering from a particularly unpleasant skin condition. We can call her Betty.

Betty lived with her parents, worked in a bank and was a regular communicant member of the Church of England. She was also a picture of misery.

One day after Church I asked her if she would like to talk about whatever it was that troubled her and she arranged to come to see me. She told me she had not been at all well. She had been in hospital with vulvitis (inflammation and irritation of the genital area) and the treatment there had not seemed to help in any way. Her mental condition was bad – she was forgetful, unable to concentrate, completely unhopeful, acutely unhappy, afraid of going mad.

Subsequently I spent an hour talking with her family doctor and we both felt that there was an underlying anxiety condition which needed to be recognised and healed. We agreed that I should try to help her. In all I saw her eight times for about an hour and a half on each occasion. There was a break in the middle of these interviews whilst she saw a psychiatrist, but the psychiatrist suggested that she should come back to me. Month by month we talked about her life – her childhood, her relationship with her parents, her fears, her loneliness. We found she was very much afraid of sex – afraid of marriage, of intercourse, of childbirth. My wife joined in some of the discussions and gradually as Betty came to trust us she admitted to us and to herself the roots of her fears, which lay in some rather unpleasant childhood experiences.

We spoke a great deal about the nature of Christian security, founded on the love of God and his acceptance of us and identification with us. Each interview ended with prayer, a blessing and the laying on of hands. At every point the family doctor knew what was happening.

Gradually both the vulvitis and the underlying anxiety lessened their grip. There was an interim period during which Betty would be free from the vulvitis for a day or two and then it would return. It would come and go and we could actually recognise the various anxiety stimulants which produced it and the positive thought patterns which soothed it away. Finally it cleared. Now many years later Betty is a happy, well-adjusted wife and mother. It was a seal upon her healing when one day she said, 'If ever it would help anybody else for you to tell them about me, I shan't mind.'

It was good to be in contact with the medical profession throughout all this. Betty's condition was such a delicate one that I would not have been happy unless I had medical contacts. I still have letters from Betty's family doctor and from the psychiatrist to whom he sent her. They both approved the treatment which I was giving. In addition I spoke to the gynaecologist who treated her in hospital and to another psychiatrist for a second opinion. It was all very much a team effort. When Betty's self revelations looked as though they might be somewhat traumatic the psychiatrist prescribed suitable tablets. When Betty's parents, who were not altogether in sympathy with the Church at that time, expressed disquiet the family doctor visited them and allayed their fears. My wife was able to play her part all the more effectively because she is a trained physiotherapist who has specialised in antenatal care. We all worked together.

Medical and spiritual treatment often go hand in hand. A clerical colleague recently told me that on a visit to a local hospital he was asked to pray with a patient who was semi-conscious and very restive and troubled. He prayed briefly and administered a laying on of hands. The patient at once went to sleep. He had been under drugs for four days but

3

only at that point did they become properly operative. The medical needed the spiritual to complete it.

Perhaps I may add a further rather personal example. A month before I wrote this chapter my wife's father died. He went into hospital for an operation, apparently survived the operation well, but died three days later, suddenly, from a heart attack. When my wife and I reached her mother, we found that not only was she very shaken by events at the hospital but also she was steadily becoming covered from head to foot in ugly painful lumps and blotches. The doctor said it was an allergy of some kind. He prescribed tablets. They had no effect. He added a prescription for ointment. It made no difference. He changed the treatment from tablets to medicine. The condition became worse than ever and it was decided to try the tablets again. At this point I had a strong urge to pray with my mother-in-law and to administer a laying on of hands in the name of Christ. It was late at night, but I went to her bedroom, and asked if she would allow me to do so. She said she had been trying to pluck up courage to ask me to do so all day, so we spent five or ten minutes in prayer and then I put my hands on her head and commended her to the healing power of our Lord. Next morning the condition had started to improve. By the time that the funeral took place thirty-six hours later, the condition was so much better that none of the mourners would have noticed anything had been wrong. The tablets, it seemed, were at last doing her good, but there was no sign whatsoever that they were doing so until she received a laying on of hands in the name of Christ. Again the spiritual complemented and completed the medical.

Betty's family doctor told me that as quite a junior G.P. he had learned the importance of an element in healing which was not strictly medical. He was called to the bedside of a poorly old lady whom he knew well and who trusted and respected him completely. As he entered the room she said, 'I shall feel better now, doctor,' and as he sat by her bedside holding her hand her racing pulse slowed down under his fingers until it became absolutely normal. He realised at that point that there was no medical reason for the improvement in the condition which was taking place before his eyes and under his hands. He said to me that he knew in that moment that there was more to healing than pills and a stethoscope.

If the presence and the touch of a trusted family doctor

can do so much, how much more can the presence and touch of Christ. Healing by touch is an old and honoured form of therapy. Every mother knows it by instinct. Many a doctor learns it from experience. It is sad that the Church has forgotten or disregarded it to such an extent for so long in spite of the evidence around us and in spite of the specific injunction of Christ.

Sometimes of course when a local church arouses itself to take an interest in Christian healing after years of comparative inactivity in this sphere, local doctors may regard the development with suspicion. There may be various reasons for this. One is that they just are not used to it. Another, that they may have come across fringe sects doing strange things – Jehovah's Witnesses refusing to allow their children to receive blood transfusions or Christian Scientists refusing drugs or other remedies or spiritualists practising so-called 'psychic surgery'. Doctors may not realise that these bodies are as unorthodox *theologically* as they are *medically*. And of course a third reason is that doctors, like the rest of us, are not free from prejudice. Christian healing may arouse it.

If we come across suspicion on the part of doctors we should be patient, be ready to explain the point and practice of Christian healing not just in terms of scripture but in terms of reason and experience, be ready to deal with objections carefully and in detail. When the moment comes that we are offered the opportunity to co-operate in healing we must take it with both hands.

In Hyde some of the doctors at the Health Centre were suspicious when we started our services of 'Investigation into Christian Healing'. One church member who went to see her doctor was told, 'Why come here? Why not go to that healing service of yours?' and at the Mission of Teaching and Healing, although the physiotherapists from the local clinic were well represented not a single doctor from the Health Centre attended any of the meetings so far as we could see. However gradually doctors are coming to see that we are not claiming any magical powers. There is no mumbo-jumbo. Nobody is being harmed and many are being helped.

It was a great day when a doctor first told one of his patients, 'I think you should go to the St George's service of healing.' As it was when a doctor phoned me and said, 'I think that perhaps you can help such and such a patient better than I can. May I arrange an appointment for her to see you?' I was delighted when two doctors came to the vicarage for an evening to discuss the whole concept of Christian healing, and even more delighted when the same two doctors subsequently attended one of our 'Rediscovery of Christian Healing' services. As they left one of them commented to a sidesman, 'I hope I shall be a better doctor for being here tonight.' Before I started to write this chapter, one of my congregation phoned me to tell me of a splendid piece of concern and healing on the part of that doctor. I hope I shall be a better pastor for having heard of that! We can help and encourage each other so much, we who have the privilege of serving the healing professions. That is the way it should be.

CHAPTER EIGHT

The Healing of Relationships

It cannot be said too often that Christian healing is not just concerned with the body but with man as a totality, life as a whole. It follows that it must be concerned with the healing of relationships.

I remember once spending the early hours of the morning with a couple who had attended one of our Christian healing services and had received the laying on of hands. They had a fair enough marriage but like many married couples they irritated each other in various ways. Each bottled up a sense of irritation at the other, but each was blissfully unaware of the irritation caused to the other. After the service the wife felt moved to uncork the bottle and tell her husband of the ways in which he irritated her. He returned the compliment. The exchange became more and more heated. In the end he became so angry that he smashed a vase which had been given them as a wedding present. She went to bed sobbing and threatening divorce. The husband sat for half an hour gazing at the fragments of the vase and wondering how in the world all this could have followed a service of healing! Then he telephoned me and asked me to go round.

We sat around the bed, he in his shirt sleeves, she in her night dress. He told me what she had said about him. She told me what he had said about her. 'Are they true, these things you have heard about yourselves?' I asked. And here the grace of God showed itself. Quite simply they both said, 'Yes.' 'And have you loved each other over the years?' I asked. 'We don't talk about that sort of thing,' they said. 'Have you loved each other?' I persisted. 'Yes,' they admitted. 'Tell each other so,' I commanded, highly autocratic. 'I've loved her. I still do,' said the husband. 'Don't tell me, tell your wife,' I said. And hesitantly, gropingly he started to speak to her of his love, and she did the same. Putting my best quasi-medical manner on, I prescribed that they should say, 'I love you' at least once a week for the rest of their lives and I threatened to check up on it.

They have almost had a second honeymoon since then. There are two new elements in their marriage – articulated love and absolute honesty. Before I left we all prayed and it was remarkable to hear them acknowledging and thanking God for the healing and deepening of their relationship. The marriage is now one of the strongest I know.

There was a similar healing in the life of 'Tess' who received the laying on of hands at one of our services. It felt, she told me later, as though the hands on her head were red hot, burning her like coals. Next month she came again. Two different people were administering the laying on of hands, but again the hands were red hot. She prayed about it and came to the conclusion that there was something in her life which God wanted to purge, to burn away. It was her normal custom to justify herself. 'They're all out of step but our Tess,' was her motto. But now honestly and thoroughly she examined herself – and she admitted the result to me and to her husband. 'I'm so ashamed,' she said, but almost under our eyes healing was taking place. She is more of a whole person now and her marriage is the better for it.

Of course we ought not to rely on 'red-hot' hands to produce this result in every case. There are many ways in which the Church can be a channel of healing. Pre-marriage preparation, honest life-centred preaching, and the family life of the Church as a whole should be geared to be helpful and healing in the sphere of marriage relationships.

Another area of relationships in which there is often need for healing is the attitude which we have to our parents, even to parents now dead. A wrong attitude to parents can underlie many a mentally or physically sick condition. Judy was a young wife who seemed incapable of getting up before eleven in the morning and never started her housework till four in the afternoon. Underneath this practice was a stressed and sick attitude to her mother, now dead. 'I loathed my mother,' she said. 'She was domineering, house-proud without having anything to be proud about, a magistrate, always giving orders, always so superior. She took all the guts out of me.' Whether this was a true picture or not, that was how Judy saw it. And there was no healing for her till she had forgiven her mother. There was Agnes who had a marriage problem. Behind it was the memory of her father who used to walk around the house naked and had a sexual attitude to her and asked her to masturbate him after she was about eight years old.

To a young child, mother and father are like gods, the source of life, love, sustenance, standards, and security. But people are not perfect. Parents are flawed gods. We all have much to thank our parents for, but we all have something to forgive them for also. Thanking and forgiving in correct proportions, demoting parents from gods to human beings like ourselves, this is part of growing into maturity. Spiritual healing is sometimes needed before we can achieve it.

Christ wants to touch our relationship with our neighbours too. But, like other forms of Christian healing, he never forces it upon us. Perhaps I may include a cautionary tale here. In a parish where I used to work there were two women who could not stand each other. One had a dog which had bitten the other one's son. She justified it by saying that her dog was a very good judge of character! The relationship had gone from bad to worse. I brought them into church, asked them to kneel down, and suggested that they each forgave each other and asked each other's forgiveness. But it was *my* bright idea, not theirs. They did not want it at all. Within ten minutes one had called on me, the other had telephoned to say, 'That woman didn't mean a word of it.' There was no healing at all. You cannot preach the gospel at the point of a gun. You cannot bring healing to those who are determined not to be healed.

I suppose this is why the healing power of Christ is not more evident in inter-class and inter-group relationships within society. Christ has his hand stretched out to heal, but we have not yet come to the point where we want his healing. We hold on to our own greed and sectional interests. We can see that something is wrong but we have not yet come to the point of repentance, the point of making ourselves available and accessible to Christ's healing power.

There are however signs that this may be beginning to happen within the Church itself. I have already written about the new unity which our mission of teaching and healing brought to some of the churches in our area. At one meeting following the mission a key member of a local free evangelical church stood up and said he now realised he had been sick for years. The name of the sickness was prejudice. For years he had supposed that the gospel was the sole property of his own church. He had thought of the Church of England as hostile to or at any rate irrelevant to the gospel. He wanted to tell us how wrong he had been and how much joy he now felt in the new friendship we were sharing.

I particularly remember sitting in a car with the vicar of a neighbouring church. Each of us was moved to admit how much had been wrong with the relationship between our churches and ourselves. From that time on the relationship has been healed.

So often the division between one church and another, the disunity amongst denominations, is not primarily theological but sociological and downright sin-centred, based on pride, prejudice and pre-conditioning. The power of Christian healing can work wonders here. If we allow forces of healing to grow in the Church, we shall see a new unity, a new strength and a new capacity for bringing the healing of relationships to our sick society.

CHAPTER NINE

The Healing of Anxiety

When Bishop Taylor Smith was asked to write something in an autograph book, he often used to write this:

> The worried cow would have lived till now
> If she had saved her breath,
> But she feared her hay wouldn't last all day
> And she mooed herself to death!

I am told that the word 'worry' comes from an Anglo-Saxon word meaning 'wolf'. Certainly worry can be like a wolf in the way it tears at life. Not that it tears the troubles from tomorrow. What it does is to tear the strength and peace from today.

Anxiety is useless, dangerous and very common. Our age has been called 'the age of anxiety'. So if the Christian Church has a Gospel for today, a Gospel which heals, it must be seen to speak relevantly and effectively to the many folk who are fettered by anxiety.

There are two types of anxiety. First there is anxiety about a specific object. Bishop Taylor Smith's worried cow knew what she was worrying about and so do many anxious men and women. 'Will I get the job I want?' 'Will I pass my exam?' 'Will I be all right when I go into hospital?' 'Are my children all right, now they are living away from home?' — and so on.

Secondly there is another sort of anxiety, a deeper sort, which does not seem to have a specific object at all. 'Milly' comes into my mind. She is a natural worrier. She has to have something to worry about. If there is no handy problem around, she will invent something, because the worry is deep inside her. Or I think of 'Poppy' who because she is deep-down anxious cannot bear to be ignored. She has to be the centre of attention. At first glance she looks self-confident, but those who know her well can see that behind the attention-seeking there is deep anxiety which cannot face being really alone. Then there is 'Alexander' who is afraid of deep friendships, afraid of being hurt and so always keeps his distance. He looks self-sufficient, but underneath it all he is not secure enough to trust another person. One day his self-sufficiency may crack, and if that happens he will be in for a nervous breakdown.

Deep insecurity is common, commoner than one might think, because we do not like to admit it and so we try to hide it, even from ourselves. But of course hiding something does not make it go away. The anxiety lurks under the surface and affects our behaviour in strange and painful ways.

How specifically can the healing power of Christ be brought to bear on an anxiety condition? Anxiety about a specific object, though it can be agonising, is the easier sort to deal with. The rule of thumb which my wife and I worked out when our younger son was ill as a baby was –

> Do your best
> And leave the rest
> to God.

This means taking the best practical action humanly possible, but at the same time putting the whole situation, including the ultimate outcome, in the hands of God. On a number of occasions people who have received a laying on of hands at one of our services have reported afterwards, 'I had this or that problem before the service but now I have decided not to worry about it any more. I'll do what I can and then leave it with God.'

It reminds me of King Hezekiah taking the sneering menacing letter which he had received from Sennacherib the Assyrian (in the second Book of Kings, chapter 20) and spreading it out in the house of the Lord before God. In effect he prayed, 'Lord you are very great and very strong. Take this situation into your hands. I'll do what I can but I will leave the issue with you.' It was a powerful prayer then. It is a powerful prayer now.

But what when we do not have a letter to spread before God? What when there is no external problem which we can commit to him – but just an inner emptiness? This sort of faceless anxiety can dominate and ruin life. How does the Christian Faith offer healing here?

I believe there is a basic threefold truth which we need to

appropriate for ourselves. God made me. God loves me. God wants me. He made me and no creation of his is valueless. He loves me even to the point of the cross. He wants me and he has something for me to do and to be in his service. There is a deep healing power in this threefold truth. I watched it, for instance, healing Betty, the girl whose skin condition concealed an underlying anxiety state. I watched it healing 'Edwina', a nervous middle-aged woman who could hardly look life or her husband in the face because of her feelings of anxiety and worthlessness. Her husband thought much more of her when she began to think more of herself. And speaking personally one of the joys of my life has been that of seeing my own deep anxiety lift from my shoulders as the threefold truth has become more and more a part of me.

The healing is a gradual process. Anxiety tends to be a deeply ingrained element in our personality with roots going back to the earliest months of life, perhaps even to the birth process itself. There is good news here and bad news. The good news is that Jesus has revealed a God who made, loves and wants us. There is healing and hope. The bad news is that the healing can be expected to take time, it may even take a lifetime. That is almost the whole story – almost, but not quite. There is a postscript which can come as a personal miracle to the anxiety sufferer.

It is usual to think of anxiety as an enemy, and so it is. But when the enemy is offered to God, it has a strange way of turning into a friend. As St Paul says, 'All things work together for good for those who love God' – even anxiety.

There are at least three ways in which God uses anxiety for our good, whilst he is gently and steadily healing it, loving it away. First, anxiety when it is recognised and accepted and offered to God can be a bulwark against the worst of all sins, the sin of pride, the folly of supposing that I can lead an adequate life centred on myself. Every twinge of anxiety can be a signal to me that man finds rest only in God.

Secondly, anxiety can help me to understand others, to stand where they stand. For there are precious few people totally unscarred by it.

Thirdly, those who know they are anxious can, I believe, experience the companionship of Christ in a unique way. On the cross Christ cried those mysterious words, 'My God, my God, why hast thou forsaken me?' God was his whole being, Christ knew what it was to lose his being in dread and dereliction. If we have to enter into the deep pains of anxiety, however deeply we may go, Christ will always have penetrated more deeply. He offers himself as our companion on the way, our guide, our fellow sufferer. The companionship of Christ is, to my knowledge, the most precious gift in the world. It may well be that within eternity those who have known the deepest anxiety in Christ's companionship will be regarded as the most fortunate of all.

Perhaps this gives some clue to the meaning of the first Beatitude. 'Blessed are the poor in spirit (literally 'those whose spirits are full of cringing fear!') for (incredibly!) THEIRS is the KINGDOM OF HEAVEN.'

CHAPTER TEN

Case history of an angry man

I shall never forget Greg. He used to sit near the back of the church. He turned up week by week, never really looking happy, sometimes looking positively depressed. He stopped coming for a while but started again – still looking depressed. One day as I looked through my window I saw him pacing up and down on the road outside. He did this for several minutes and rather belatedly it struck me that he was pluck-ing up courage to come and talk to me. I went to the front door and simultaneously he must have found his courage because we met there. 'I don't know why I've come,' he said. 'You can't help me. Nobody can.' I invited him in and he came into my study where he sat for minutes without saying anything, his head in his hands.

In the end he spoke. 'I feel so rotten and ill,' he said. He told me he had feelings of tension in his head, he could not breathe properly because his nose was continually congested, he had a tight feeling across his chest, his heart bumped away, he sweated all the time (he was certainly sweating at the moment), he could not sleep at night, he could not con-centrate by day, his finger nails were bitten down, he looked as though the world was on his shoulders.

Gradually he started to talk about his life. By any stan-dards he had not had the easiest of lives. When he was thirteen years old his mother died. When he was eighteen his father died. When he was nineteen he married a lovely girl, the apple of his eye. She died of cancer when he was twenty-three. He had married again but now his second wife, like his first, had become ill, and seemed not to be making pro-gress. He had had a series of unsatisfactory jobs. In one of them there was an accounting error and he came under suspicion. Although he was completely cleared he felt he had to leave. In his present job he did not get on with his head of department. Because of feeling ill, his standard of work had

45

slipped and his superior had reprimanded him. He was afraid he might be sacked. He had gone to his doctor, but his doctor told him there was nothing wrong with him and he must pull himself together. He had always gone to church and believed in a God of the ten commandments, a God of judgement. He did not enjoy church, but on the one occasion on which he stopped he was involved in a road accident and ended up in a ditch, which he took as a warning from God. He could see no way out of his ill health, his problems at home, his problems at work – except perhaps one.

On a hunch I asked him if he had ever thought of putting an end to it all. He covered his face again and admitted that he thought of suicide more and more.

By this time we had spent nearly two hours together and I felt the need to think and pray. I asked him to come again at a set time the next day and made him promise that until then at any rate he would put aside thoughts of suicide. I also told him that he had been right to come to me and that a solution to his troubles might be nearer than he thought.

Next day it seemed right to feed the situation back to him and to interpret it to some extent. On the surface he looked depressed and burdened. But underneath it he must, I felt, be suppressing a great deal of anger. This is often so in cases of depression and I wanted to see if I could bring it into the open.

'I'm not surprised,' I said, 'that you are feeling fed up with life. If I were you I'd be smouldering about it. Just think . . .' and I led him back through the death of his mother, his father and his first wife, his wife's illness, the unfair treatment in his former job, the unfair treatment in his present job.

'Do you know,' I said innocently, 'if you bottle up this sort of anger it can make you feel ill in all sorts of ways?' I took down a text book from a shelf and started reading a list of the sort of symptoms which suppressed anger can produce – head tension, nasal congestion, tightness of the chest, heart fast and bumpy, sweating, insomnia. They were all his symptoms.

At this point, for the first time he let his anger out and he directed it initially against his doctor. He stood up and strode about the room. For a time I thought he was going to break something. He was so furious. 'That bloody doctor,' he shouted, 'he should have known, he should have told me.'

I let him rage away for a time and then said, 'Perhaps you

are right to be cross about your doctor, but face it, you're not just angry with your doctor, you're angry with life itself.' He admitted it. 'And that means,' I said, 'that you're angry with GOD.'

Suddenly he was quiet. He did not like this as an idea because his idea of God was of a hard, judgement god, a god of rules, regulations and requirements, a god who knocks you into a ditch if you stop going to church for a while. However I was able to show him that sort of god was a god in his own head, not the God revealed to us by Jesus. I took him to the cross and we saw together that even when we ram down the crown of thorns and knock in the nails Christ goes on loving and that this is what God is like. I encouraged him to take his anger and his total experience of life to the cross and leave them there. We prayed and I administered a laying on of hands.

Soon after Greg attended an evangelistic service and on the basis of his new-found understanding of himself and of God he went forward as an act of commitment to the true God whom he was beginning to know and trust.

I saw him for a final interview about a fortnight later. He was a changed man. His depression had gone. His health troubles had gone. His concentration was back. His superior at work was so surprised by the change in his work that he checked to see whether his other colleagues were doing it for him! 'I wouldn't have thought it possible that I could be so changed,' he said. We thanked God for it together. Two years later he left the parish, but before going he came to see me and said very simply, 'Before I go I want to tell you that you have saved my life.'

I have told this story in detail because it takes us to the heart of Christian healing. Underlying Greg's bodily symptoms, his feelings of depression, his difficulties in dealing with the people around him and in coping with life as a whole was the fact that he was not right with God. His relationship with God needed healing. This was also true of Betty, Tess, Judy, Agnes, Milly, Poppy, Alexander and in one sense or another of us all. The heart of Christian healing lies not in the treatment of bodily ailments no matter how painful or tragic they may be. Basically it does not even lie in correcting man's attitude to his fellow man or man's attitude to himself, though in a fallen world both are wrong and sick. The deepest purpose of Christian healing is to right the relationship between

man and God. Our wrong relationship with God is the ill
which underlies all others. The heart of Christian wholeness
lies in right-relatedness to God.

The healing work of Christ and the healing work of
Christ's church is to minister wholeness and harmony with
God to a divided and discordant world. The place from
which this healing flows is supremely the cross of Christ – the
cross on which he died and from which he rose triumphant.
'By his stripes we are healed.' Greg found this true in his own
experience. We can all find it true.

From the cross Christ offers us the saving relationship
within which he bears the consequences of our sins and our
rages, shares the depths of our anxieties and our fears, and
tends the hurts of our bodies, minds and spirits. Each healing
experience of the Cross is unique, created by God with pre-
cision to bring forgiveness for our own individual sins, to meet
perfectly our own individual needs, and to restore in us that
aspect of the image of God which is our true self.

CHAPTER ELEVEN

A glimpse of Jesus

The object of the sermon at our 'Rediscovery of Christian Healing' service is always quite simply that of seeing and hearing Jesus. There can be no Christian healing without genuine contact with Christ. The text which comes to mind again and again is, 'Sir, we would see Jesus.' It virtually comes before my eyes as I preach. There has to be real contact and it has to be with the real Christ. There are many common false notions about Christ and false pictures of him. If the word at these services is truly to be his word and the touch truly his touch these false ideas about Jesus must be dispelled.

For instance there is the picture of Christ as a pale, unreal, stained glass window type of figure, whom you could never imagine sweating or laughing or living anything which could be recognised as ordinary life. There is no incarnation here and little healing. It is the product of bogus pietism. Or there is the idea, perhaps founded on a wrong interpretation of 'Gentle Jesus, meek and mild,' of a 'sissy' Christ, who wouldn't say boo to a goose. Jesus could be gentle of course, but he could also take a scourge and drive those who were commercialising and exploiting religion out of the temple.

There is the middle class respectable Christ, who comforts and buttresses conventional prejudice. That sort of Jesus does not accord with the evidence of scripture. The real Jesus made it plain that he did not come to call the 'respectable' (Luke 5: 32) and the leading citizens made it plain that they wanted to be rid of him (Luke 19: 47).

Or by contrast there is the left-wing 'Che Guevara' guerrilla-type Christ, a political revolutionary, who would have had no sympathy with the respect which the real Jesus showed for civic and religious authority, and would not have wasted his time loving his enemies.

There is the narrow-minded bigoted Christ who would never have gone to parties and who would have been keener to turn wine into water than vice-versa. It is a startling thought that when the enemies of Jesus wanted to throw insults at him they called him a 'glutton and a wine-bibber!' (Matthew 11: 19).

And there is the popular picture of Jesus as a good and kind home-spun philosopher – whom nobody could possibly have wanted to crucify! – a sentimental rather than a scriptural Christ.

So what type of man was Jesus? The answer is that he defies type-casting. He was himself. The only way to answer the question, 'What was Jesus like?' is to look at the evidence and let him speak for himself.

This is why at our service of 'Rediscovery of Christian Healing' we hand out copies of St Luke's Gospel and work through it chapter by chapter, verse by verse, the hard parts as well as the easy parts, the uncongenial parts as well as those we happen to like. The object is to see Jesus as he was and as he is. This sort of preaching is not only full of surprises and full of healing for a congregation, it is also highly salutary for the preacher because most preachers tend to be selective in approaching scripture and it is good to accept a framework which specifically excludes pre-selection and the distortion which can come with it.

This is a good point to stop talking about looking at Jesus and start actually doing it for a while. So here is a random passage from St Luke's Gospel and some of the thoughts which it brought to us when we considered it at a service. The passage is from Luke, chapter 5, verses 12–32.

Jesus has just called the first disciples and they have heard the call, left everything, and followed him. Characteristically their first experience as followers is to see and marvel at Jesus as a healer.

'While he was in one of the towns Jesus came across a man who was full of leprosy' – not necessarily someone whom modern doctors would describe as a leper, because the ancient world called various skin conditions leprosy. But the condition, whatever it was, was a serious and clearly visible one. He was full of it, says St Luke, using the terminology which a doctor of those times would naturally employ. Poor man, physically he was a mess, socially he would be an outcast. All lepers were made to feel unwanted and unclean. Indeed the insecurity and lack of love could well have been an element in the condition. 'When he saw Jesus he fell to the ground, face in the dust, and begged him, "Lord, if you want to, you can make me clean." Jesus stretched out his hand, touched the leper, and said, "Certainly I want to. Be clean." '

The man did not doubt the power of Christ to heal, but he doubted the will of Christ to heal. This may seem strange but it still sometimes happens. It was how the housewife with the phobic condition in chapter four felt. She accepted without question that Christ could heal her. The object of the counselling session was to make the point that she was precious to him and that he not only could heal her but longed to do so. Once she had accepted this the healing process had begun.

The touch of Christ upon the leper was a symbol of acceptance and security, powerful in the case of any ailment, but particularly powerful in conditions which render the sufferer socially unacceptable.

'Immediately the leprosy left him.' The immediacy may surprise us, but skin conditions can react very quickly. We have seen how Betty the girl with the vulvitis found that at one stage of her experience of healing her skin condition changed from day to day. Even more startling was the case of Janette, a young woman with an ugly skin condition which affected her hands, a condition which actually changed before my eyes as I was counselling her.

'Jesus instructed the leper to tell nobody. He said, "Show yourself to the priest and make the sacrifice prescribed by Moses, as evidence to the authorities." ' Normally Jesus tried to avoid publicity for his healings, and following this practice we have never advertised a Service of Healing, except in connection with the Mission of Teaching and Healing. Note the respect of Jesus for the old traditional ways of Leviticus, chapters 13 and 14, even though he himself was introducing new dimensions of life and healing to his followers.

In spite of his injunction to the leper – 'the news about him spread all the more. Great crowds collected to hear him and he healed them of their diseases. Jesus on his part made a practice of slipping away to deserted places for prayer.' And if he felt the need of prayer, how much more should we feel it in a ministry of healing. An important element in our local service consists of silent prayer undertaken by a group of worshippers beforehand in church. As others enter the building, they enter an atmosphere of prayer.

'One day when Jesus was teaching, some Pharisees and

teachers of the law were sitting there. They had come from
every town in Galilee, Judaea and Jerusalem. God's power to
heal people was with him.' It seems that this was not always
necessarily so. Jesus could experience blocks to healing, just
as we do. 'Some men arrived carrying a paralytic man on a
bed and tried to bring him in and put him down in front of
Jesus. The crowd was so great that they were not able to
find a way in.' In the story of the leper, the man had faith
himself, but in the case of the paralytic it is friends who have
faith. The crowd following Jesus was an actual hindrance
here. I wonder how often those of us who reckon to follow
Jesus are in fact an obstacle, blocking the way of others rather
than helping them along the way.

The friends of the paralytic man were not put off by difficulties. 'They went up on to the roof of the house, took off
some tiles, and let him down, bed and all, in the middle of the
crowd in front of Jesus.' This really was friendship. Faith,
friendship, foresight, flexibility and fortitude, we can find
them all in the attitude of these men. At our services we find
people with a similar persevering faith, working and praying
for the healing of others.

'And when Jesus saw their faith – the faith of the friends –
he said to the paralysed man, "My friend, your sins are forgiven." ' Paralysis can be caused by guilt. Where this is so it
can be dangerous to heal the paralysis without treating the
guilt. Jesus recognised that this was the case here.

Note the underlying claim to authority in the words of
Jesus. The scribes and Pharisees were certainly quick to see
it. They seemed to have little concern for the paralysed man
himself but they pounced on the theological issue. 'They
began to argue. They said, "Who is this man who speaks
blasphemy? Who can forgive sins? Only God!" ' They saw
the problem and were close to the solution, but they rejected
it.

'Jesus knew what was going on in their minds' – just as he
knew the guilt of the paralysed man and the faith of the
friends, and just as he knows your depths and mine. 'Which is
easier,' he asked, 'to say, "Your sins are forgiven you", or to
say, "Get up and walk"?' There was no answer. The process
of heart-hardening which was to be so obvious later in his
ministry was beginning already. To demonstrate that he did
in fact have the authority to forgive sins Jesus 'commanded
the paralytic man, "Take up your bed and go home".' I

would not dare to do this. My perception is not sharp enough.
The flow of healing which comes through me is not sufficiently concentrated. But Jesus knew what he was doing.
'Instantly the paralysed man stood up in front of everybody,
picked up the bed on which he had been lying and went
home, praising God. Everyone was caught up in astonish-
ment. They were full of awe and praised God. "We have seen
incredible things today," they said.' The man praised God.
The crowd praised God. The praise was as much a part of the
miracle as the cure. Praising God and wholeness before God
go together.

There is one further story of healing in the passage we are
considering. At first sight it may not seem to be about healing,
but Christian healing is not concerned exclusively, nor even
primarily, with the body. 'Afterwards Jesus went out and
looked at a tax collector,' and we know that Jesus had
remarkable eyes, 'he looked at Levi, as he sat at his tax col-
lection desk.' Tax collectors worked for the Roman occupying
forces. They made a fat living by keeping part of the takings
for themselves. They were known as cheats and traitors and
were hated. 'Jesus said, "Follow me." ' Surprisingly, 'Levi got
up, left everything, and followed him.' Jesus was in the process of turning one who had probably been a greedy, shady
materialist into a man of God. Perhaps the most spectacular
healing so far!

See what followed. 'Then Levi gave a big reception for
Jesus at his house, and there was a great crowd of tax collectors and others with them at the feast.' Levi had a ball.
Accepting Christ's spiritual healing brings tremendous happiness. But the scribes and Pharisees were not happy. They
muttered to the disciples and said, 'Why do you eat and
drink with tax collectors and sinners?' Again the heart-
hardening process was in evidence, and unlike Levi, the
scribes and Pharisees were not happy. There is no joy in
resisting Christian insight and healing. Jesus took their muttered question seriously and answered them. 'It is not healthy
people who need a doctor but ill people. My purpose is to
call sinners to repentance not to spend time with those who
think themselves already good enough.' The Church is not a
club for people with delusions of superiority. It is a hospital
for sinners. Its business is healing at every level, just as this
was the business of Jesus.

This has been no more than a glimpse of Jesus, twenty-one

verses from one of the gospels. It is about as much as can be
fitted into a single service. But even a single glimpse of Jesus
has healing in it and month by month glimpses of Jesus can
build up into a good look at him. You may have heard the
story of the old man who used to tell people that he
reckoned he had been saved by having good looks. When
anyone queried the statement he expanded it by saying the
good looks which save are good looks at Jesus – 'Looking to
Jesus the author and perfector of our faith.'

Good looks at the good Lord – this is of the essence of the
receipt of life and health from Christ and it must be of the
essence of the message at any service of Christian healing.

CHAPTER TWELVE

Death

Greta was in the final stages of cancer. A colostomy had given her a few months of extra life but it was a dubious mercy. Her body was wasted and ulcerous. She was never free from pain. And as if this were not enough her mental suffering matched the physical pain. Tension was written all over her face. She could not relax nor let her relatives relax. Though life was unbearable, the prospect of death was even more so. Nobody dared to mention it, even as a possibility.

One of the family asked me to call and I visited Greta twice during the last fortnight of her life. We talked a little about her life, her home, her family — and then I broached the forbidden subject. 'One of these days we're all going to die,' I said. 'Normally we don't think about it all that much, but I suppose a serious illness like this makes you start to think about it and to wonder about it.' To begin with she denied it, but I went on as gently as I could, 'Well, you may find that the moment comes. In my job I have to think about it a great deal. I don't have any choice. The thing which makes it bearable is knowing that Christ is not only with me in life but he will be with me in death and he can cope with both.' Gradually we began to talk about Jesus as the Lord of life and Conqueror of death. We spoke of his saving and healing work in life and in death. We prayed together and I administered a laying on of hands in the name of Christ.

When I saw her a week later she had changed. She said that the pain was less severe and that her ulcer did not need to be dressed as often, but the most noticeable thing was that the tension had gone from her face. She was learning to rest in the presence of God, to trust him, to leave the issue of life and death in his hands. She had asked for a Bible and now read it every day. Her family noticed the difference in many ways. They were now allowed to sleep through the night without being continually called to see to her wants. The atmosphere was no longer brittle and forced. I actually enjoyed my last hour with Greta. She died a few days later.

There is such a thing as a 'healed death'. It is a privilege to witness it and to share the insights which it brings. It can have dignity and even beauty. It can reach out and touch the lives of those around, who paradoxically in the observation of death can begin to experience the stirrings of new dimensions of life.

I think of Dora, a deeply committed Christian woman, who developed a cancer which distorted her body and caused her terrible pain. Week by week I visited her. We talked together and prayed together. I laid hands on her and longed for her healing, but though she told me that the laying on of hands often brought a period of freedom from pain, physical healing did not follow. Her courage and her faith were undying but her body was not.

Her death saddened the whole church, the whole neighbourhood. Why did she die? Why was there no physical healing after regular prayer and regular laying on of hands? I wish I knew. However the situation was not without healing. I could feel the power of her love and her faith and so could others. After her death her husband and son and daughter-in-law began to come to church week by week. They came with enquiring minds and a readiness to learn. Dora had longed for it for years before her death, but it was only in and through her death that it began to happen.

It must infuriate Satan when death itself is used as a weapon against him! It happened supremely, of course, in the death of Jesus. It happened when early Christians chose to die in the Roman arenas rather than betray their Lord and their Faith. Martyrdoms throughout the centuries have released the power of God, and at an ordinary domestic level whenever a Dora or a Greta offers death trustingly to the Lord, God's healing grace is enabled to flow.

Now a word about funerals. Every year the Church is immensely privileged to have the opportunity to minister to millions of families going through times of bereavement and mourning. It may no longer be as common as it used to be to send for a clergyman in cases of impending death, but it is still normal practice to invite a clergyman to conduct a service after a death. This is a tremendous opportunity. I have no doubts whatsoever that every funeral service is a potential service of Christian healing and should be regarded as such.

The fact that it is not usual to think of a funeral service in this way is, I believe, the greatest single missed opportunity in the Church today.

Think for a moment of the situation at a typical funeral. For a time, even if a restricted time, there is a genuine openness to the challenge of spiritual reality. There are real hurts to be healed, real doubts to be faced, real questions to be answered. People come to the service wondering whether the Christian Faith really can make a difference to life and death or whether the whole funeral will be meaningless. They come with a mixture of pain and guilt, anger, anxiety and confusion and for a time there is a readiness to receive spiritual truth. They wonder whether there is such a thing as life after death and whether the story of the resurrection of Jesus is fact or fairy tale. They wonder whether there is a Heaven and a Hell. Some contemplate not only the death of a loved one but their own future death and their own present way of life. Many are conscious of a sense of need, perhaps for the first time in years. Some wonder whether the parson really believes the words of the service or whether he is just going through the motions. If he has anything in his own heart which can genuinely minister to the situation, they want to know it and to test it. They often go away disappointed after complete failure of communication, complete failure of healing.

I can remember clearly the two worst funerals I ever attended. One was sentimental and maudlin. The prayer was full of negative unhelpful emotionalism. 'Be with your servant Lord, when she returns to an empty house, when she looks at the empty chair in which her loved one will never sit again, when she sees the empty slippers which he will never wear again . . . ' Almost sadistic! Then there was the 'tribute', which also served to emphasise the sense of loss. The other funeral was cold and formal. The parson rattled through the prayers in a remote, impersonal voice. There was not even a handshake afterwards. I have heard both types of funeral defended, the former on the grounds that people like a bit of emotion and expect to hear a recital of the virtues of the deceased, the latter on the grounds that bereavement is a very painful personal time and that it is an impertinence to intrude upon the privacy of the grief of those who mourn. However the fundamental criticism of both types of service must be that healing is unlikely to take place at either, because on neither occasion is Christ likely to be made real to the people.

May I suggest that those of us who conduct funerals should *always* speak simply and directly of the faith which is in us? I am not for a moment saying that this is a time for manipulating the grief and weakness of mourners in order to engineer some sort of emotional response to an evangelistic appeal. That would be unpardonable. What I am pleading for is that, having thought and prayed about a funeral, we then look the mourners in the face, sense the nature of their needs, which will never be identical in the case of any two groups of mourners, and speak simply to those needs in the name and resources of the risen Christ. If he is a healing reality in our lives, if he is making a fundamental difference to our personal experience of life and our personal attitude to death, the mourners with their momentarily sharpened sensitivity will recognise spiritual truth for what it is and lives can, and will, be touched and changed.

Several regular members of my own congregation started to come to church and to enter into a meaningful Christian experience because they first felt Christ's healing touch at a funeral service. It is a wonderful thing when a service instigated by death becomes an agency of healing and life. To see the burden lift from the face of a mourner because one has spoken Christ's healing word is one of the supreme joys of the ministry and it is a paradoxical and marvellous thing to see new life begin at a funeral.

CHAPTER THIRTEEN

Distant Healing

Some people who have no objection to the concept of a direct person-to-person ministry of Christian healing baulk at the idea of distant healing or the idea that one can receive a laying on of hands by proxy for someone else who may be many miles away. I know of a doctor who sat uneasily through a Church Council meeting whilst Christian healing was being discussed, but stood up and walked out in protest as soon as mention was made of distant healing. He felt that the discussion had moved into the realm of superstition and mumbo-jumbo.

However Jesus certainly exercised distant healing. He did not minister directly to the centurion's servant. The centurion did not expect him to do so. 'Just give the order,' he said, 'and my servant will get well' (Luke 7: 7), and that was the way it happened.

It still happens that way. One Christmas Eve my wife went into church and found a parishioner, a former hospital sister, praying there. She was in a state of considerable distress, because her teenage son had had an operation and had been sent home from hospital but his condition had deteriorated. 'I have seen patients die after operations,' she said. 'I can recognise the signs and I am afraid for my son.' I telephoned her later, after my wife had told me the story. We were due to celebrate our Christmas Eve Midnight Communion. I told her that if she wished it we would pause in the middle of the service and the whole congregation would pray for her son. She gratefully accepted.

Later she told me that as we prayed for him in church his restlessness settled, he fell into a deep sleep, and next day he was very much better and clearly on the way to recovery. A coincidence? If so there are more of them.

The vicarage telephone rang one day during a week following one of our services of Rediscovery of Christian Healing. My wife answered it and a woman's voice said, 'You don't know me, but I feel I must ring up to say thank you for Sunday's service. I came to it because I was at my wits' end. My son is seriously ill mentally. He has been receiving psychiatric treatment in and out of hospital for many months and recently he has been worse than ever. I heard about your service and came to receive a laying on of hands by proxy on his behalf and I want you to know that since then his condition has improved out of recognition. For the first time in months I can see light and hope in the situation.'

Another coincidence? Then how about this? One of our congregation was worried about a relative in the south of England who had gone into hospital for an operation, and so she received a laying on of hands by proxy for her. Later her relative told her, 'I was very upset and agitated when I went into hospital but whilst your service was taking place something strange happened to me. I experienced a great feeling of calm, which persisted afterwards. I had an excellent night and next day awoke without feelings of anxiety. I felt able to trust myself to the surgeons without fear and the operation was a complete success.' A third coincidence? One is reminded of the words of William Temple, 'I find that when I pray coincidences happen. When I cease to pray, coincidences stop happening.'

Another person in the south of England was healed of diabetes insipidus at the same time that one of our congregation was receiving a proxy laying on of hands on her behalf. Paradoxically the member of St George's who received the proxy laying on of hands herself suffered from sugar diabetes but this condition was untouched.

Perhaps I may add one further story of distant healing, a rather personal one. Last summer I was saddened to receive a letter from my mother who lives in Cornwall telling me that she was not well. She normally writes happy letters but the tone of this one was thoroughly depressed. For weeks she had been suffering from a two-fold condition in which painful sciatica was combined with a rash of ugly, irritating pustules, which resisted all attempts at treatment. As I read the letter my first reaction was to feel completely helpless, over three hundred and fifty miles away from her, but I went into my study and there quietly sought to convey some sort of distant healing to her in the name of Christ. Her next letter was an amazing transformation. The sciatica and the rash had both cleared up. 'The sky is blue and life is good,' she wrote.

There the story might have ended, another possible co-incidence to add to the list. But some weeks later, in a further letter, she felt she must tell me the details of her experience of healing. After beginning, 'I hope you won't feel I am going off my head,' she went on to say how (at about the same time at which unknown to her I was endeavouring to channel Christ's healing power to her) she felt moved to go to her bedroom. There on an impulse she touched the palm cross which I had sent her from St George's. Immediately in her mind's eye she was kneeling at the communion rail at St George's and was receiving a laying on of hands. This was administered by two people, one of whom she recognised as me, the other she felt was George Bennett, although she had never met him or seen his photograph. A sense of peace came over her and immediately her condition began to improve. Some days later she was watching television and a picture of George Bennett appeared on the screen as part of a trailer for the forthcoming programme on Christian healing from St George's church. The face was exactly the face she had seen in the mental picture she had received in her bedroom days before. It would really take a piece of mental gymnastics to attribute that to coincidence!

So in my own limited experience there are occasions on which Christian healing has taken place over a distance and without a person-to-person encounter. Others who undertake a ministry of healing tell me that the same is true also in their experience.

On reflection I cannot see that there is any reason to think distant healing a strange thing if we believe in prayer. The doctor who walked out of his Church Council when distant healing was mentioned must have prayed for people who were some distance from him. It is a commonplace of prayer to ask God's protection for and blessing upon absent friends and loved ones. God is everywhere and therefore he is a bridge in time and space between us and our loved ones. To receive a laying on of hands by proxy is an acted prayer, and if any power at all is released by prayer there is no logical reason why it should not be released by the ministry of distant healing.

CHAPTER FOURTEEN

How does Christian Healing Work?

We have looked at some of the reasons for believing in the reality and importance of Christian healing. We have looked at the breadth of its application and scope. It may now be helpful to ask how it actually works? What are its resources and its channels?

The resources which underlie Christian healing are three-fold. There are the creative energies of God the Father which have been in the universe since its genesis and which are about and in us always. There are the saving mercies of God the Son, available to us through his life, death and resurrection. There is the life giving power of God the Holy Spirit, available to all who make themselves available to him. We have already seen that there are many varied channels through which this healing can flow. Here now, listed for convenience, are nine of these channels of healing.

Perhaps the first to come to mind, though not I think the most important, is the laying on of hands in the name of Christ. Jesus himself laid hands on the sick. For instance after the healing of Peter's mother-in-law: 'After sunset, all who had friends who were sick with various diseases brought them to Jesus; he placed his hands on every one of them and healed them all' (Luke 4: 40). He promised that, 'Believers will place their hands on the sick, and they will get well.' (Mark 16: 18). It is not just the clergy who may do this. It is a ministry given to the Church as a whole. This is why at St George's, Hyde, we have involved both clergy and laity in the laying on of hands at services. Of course it should not be confined to services. The touch of Christ can be conveyed on any occasion formally or informally. It is not even necessary to say, 'I am going to administer a laying on of hands in the name of Christ.' It can happen naturally on all sorts of occasions. I administered it once on our local canal tow-path. I was out for a walk and happened to meet one of the men of the congregation who was off work with a bad back. I did not attempt to say what I was doing but as he told me where the pain was I touched each place with a silent prayer. Afterwards he told me that he knew just what I was doing even though not a word was spoken. There was an immediate improvement in his condition and he was soon back at work. If the touch is to be accompanied by an audible prayer, it must be a prayer which is right and natural for the ministrant. Jesus was able to say, 'Take up your bed and walk!' I would suggest that few of us have the spiritual perception or the flow of healing to be able to say that, except perhaps under the strongest of impulsions from the Lord on a specific occasion. But we may find words which are right for us at our particular level of spiritual development – perhaps as simple as, 'God bless you,' perhaps specifically introducing the thought of healing, 'God bless you and heal you.' In our Rediscovery of Healing we say, 'May the healing power of the Holy Spirit be in you,' sometimes varying the words to match the Church's year, saying for instance at Christmas, 'May the healing power of the Christ Child work in you.' Sometimes I adapt a blessing: 'The Lord bless you and keep you, the Lord make the light of his face shine upon you and grant you healing and peace.' Sometimes I weave a prayer around the threefold resources of Christian healing: 'May the creative energies of the Father, and the saving mercies of Jesus Christ and the life giving power of the Holy Spirit work in you and heal you from all that hurts you.'

Prayer can be a channel of healing without a laying on of hands. This is true of both public and private prayer, prayer for others and prayer for ourselves. Personally I believe that a prayer for healing should never be accompanied by the words, 'if it be thy will'. But it is equally true that we should avoid a rigid state of mind. We may not know the nature of the healing which is most needed and our rigidity may itself be a block to healing.

The spoken word can be full of healing. 'My son,' says the book of Proverbs (chapter 4, verses 20–22), 'attend to my words; incline your ear to my sayings. Let them not depart from your eyes; keep them in your heart. For they are life to those who find them, and health to all their flesh.' In the chapter on death I was pleading for 'the healing word' to be an integral part of every funeral. People sometimes say afterwards, 'I do feel better, you have made such a difference to me.' This is also the purpose of the exposition of scripture at our Rediscovery of Christian Healing services.

If it can be a healing act to speak in the name of Christ, it can also be a healing act to listen in his name. It is often said that since we have two ears and one mouth we ought to do twice as much listening as talking. There is a great deal of truth and importance in this for those who would exercise a ministry of healing. An effective counselling session, despite its name, is mostly a matter of listening. There would have been no healing for Greg and Betty and many of the other people mentioned in these pages if I had not been prepared to listen and to keep on listening. Often, oddly enough, when the healing word is spoken, it is spoken not by the counsellor but by the person being counselled. He has known it all along, but has needed to be heard out in order to come to the point of admitting it to himself.

There is healing, too, in every good relationship. If a Church is true to its calling to be the family of God, the day-to-day encounter of member with member in Christian fellowship will be rich in healing. One of our former curates has a teenage mongol son. From the start his parents have loved and accepted him and when he came to St George's the congregation did the same. It was a moving experience to see him grow and blossom under that love. He is still a mongol but he has an infectious happiness and a lively independence, both of which are the product of real Christian healing.

As far as worship is concerned it would be wrong to think that healing is confined to services of Christian healing. If the Church had not neglected Christian healing over the years, specific services of healing might not now be necessary. Healing would be a normal feature of services as a whole. We have already looked at funeral services as services of healing. Perhaps special mention should also be made of the Service of Holy Communion, the act of worship directly given to the Church by Jesus. It is a normal part of every communion service to pray for the sick and claim Christ's power to heal, and the Anglican prayer book service makes it plain that the purpose of the giving of bread and wine to each communicant is so that the body and blood of Christ may 'preserve thy body and soul to everlasting life'. It has for years seemed very natural to us to include at our midweek celebration of Holy Communion a list of the names of those sick people for whom we wish as a Church to pray, and it is not uncommon to find a communicant with tears in his or her eyes – often a sign of the healing touch of Christ.

In this list of channels of Christian healing I ought, I think, to refer to the practice of unction. We are told in St Mark's Gospel, chapter 6, verse 13, that the disciples of Jesus 'poured oil on many sick people and healed them'. James instructs Christian elders to anoint the sick with oil in the name of the Lord (James 5: 14). This is a practice which I have not so far incorporated in my own ministry of healing. In the past I have taken it that these verses contained an instruction to provide simple medical care rather than to perform a symbolic act of healing. Certainly in the story of the Good Samaritan oil was poured into the wounds of the man who fell among thieves for medical purposes and not as a spiritual symbol. Similarly Isaiah, chapter 1, verse 6, speaks of wounds being mollified with oil. However it is indisputable that many people find unction a powerful channel of Christian healing and my own practice may well change and develop in this respect.

Ordinary medical care may itself of course be a channel of Christian healing and often is so. It adds a new dimension to medical care if it is regarded by both doctors and patients as an expression of the ministry of divine healing. I have the feeling, for instance, that a pill or a medicine may well be more effective if one asks God's blessing on it (perhaps in the form of a sort of 'Grace') before taking it.

This chapter is not an attempt to produce an extensive list of channels of Christian healing, but there is perhaps one further addition which should be made to it. I think of two teenage girls – let's call them Franchette and Josephine – who came to the vicarage one day in a state of considerable agitation. They had become mixed up in a circle which dabbled in the occult and Franchette was a very troubled person in consequence. She said that everywhere she went she was dogged by the sense of an evil presence. It was, she said, as though someone or something malevolent was continually walking behind her. The two girls had both withdrawn from any practices connected with the occult, but the feeling of an evil presence persisted. Sceptics might doubt its objective reality but no one could doubt the reality of the harm it was doing to Franchette. Josephine was almost equally worried as she could see the effect which all of this was having upon her friend.

We went into church. The girls knelt at the communion rail and I stood behind it. I gave Franchette a crucifix to hold to concentrate her thoughts and I prayed, not in any set form but as the words came, thanking God for his goodness and power, thanking him for making that goodness and power available to us in Jesus Christ. I praised God for the fact that Christ is stronger than any power of evil and that the strong triumphant risen Christ was present with us there and then. I claimed his power to banish whatever it was that was troubling Franchette and prayed that God's Holy Spirit might be in her to hallow and protect her life. Franchette knelt for a while and then stood and said, 'It has gone. For the first time in weeks it isn't there any more.'

I suggested to her that she should now maintain a closeness to holy things and should worship regularly. She was from another neighbourhood and had deliberately come to a church other than her own for help because she did not want the story known by her own friends and neighbours. So I would have had no means of knowing how she fared subsequently had not Josephine written to me some time later. She put no address at the top of the letter because she, like Franchette, wanted to remain as anonymous as possible, but she said that she felt she must write to say that Franchette was now completely normal again and that there had been no recurrence of the trouble. She wanted to say how grateful they both were and that they would never again dabble in the occult.

Some might give the rather grand name of exorcism to that incident. It illustrates the point that sometimes Christian healing is not just a matter of soothing a hurt but involves rebuking and driving out an evil. It may be an evil connected in some way with the occult. It may be a spirit of fear, or a spirit of lust, or some other aspect of evil. These things can have a stranglehold upon life but Christ can break that stranglehold. The casting out of evil goes hand in hand with healing in the gospels and as the Church begins to rediscover Christian healing it is important that we should also rediscover a realistic, sensible, scriptural ministry of deliverance from evil.

CHAPTER FIFTEEN

Who needs healing?

We all need healing. Sometimes we do not realise the exact nature of our need for healing. Sometimes we actively resist that knowledge. Healing is like saving. We all need saving, but amongst men everywhere there is widespread resistance to the idea. It is easy to see that the villains of history were sinners – people like Nero or Hitler. But we are tempted to disassociate ourselves from folk like that. We say to ourselves, 'I don't commit murder or rape my neighbour's wife or rob old ladies in the street or anything like that. I'm as good as the next man.' The trouble is that he is a sinner too. We both need saving. Neither of us loves God with all his heart. Neither of us loves our neighbours as we love ourselves. If either of us were to stand beside Jesus, the light of his goodness and love would reveal us as the sinners that we are. The first step towards letting Jesus do his saving work is to let him show us that we need it.

It is much the same with healing, as one would expect, seeing 'healing' and 'saving' often translate the same Greek word in the New Testament. I remember Herbert arguing about his own need for healing. He thought it a great idea that I should go around the parish administering a laying on of hands to people who were obviously sick, but he was adamant that he did not need it. He had a bit of a cold, he said, but that was all. Apart from that he was in perfect health. A year later he came to the communion rail at a service of healing for a laying on of hands. He had thought his way through it and now saw it very differently. At a purely physical level we are rarely a hundred per cent fit, at a mental level few of us could claim to be perfectly integrated persons, and at a spiritual level we all have temptation problems. Who would be rash enough to claim that all his relationships are completely healthy? Who would be stupid enough to say that we do not live in a sick society and who would be so conceited as to claim that he personally has absolutely no part in the sickness of that society? Perfect health in body, mind and spirit, in thought, word and deed – that is what we have to claim before the healing touch of Christ will be an irrelevance to us. Herbert came to see that he could make no such claim. Now he receives the ministry of healing regularly, and it is beginning to change and heal him.

So who needs healing? We all do. I do. You do. With this in mind perhaps I may try to offer some practical thoughts to you and to myself with a view to our personal healing. If we are to experience the healing touch of Christ upon our lives in its fullness, it is important for us to cultivate a spirit of flexible availability. Rigidity is the enemy of healing.

There are two types of rigidity which commonly hinder healing. One is the rigidity of hopelessness. Every doctor knows how hard it is to bring healing to a patient who has decided his case is hopeless and has given up the will to live. The devil loves to stir up feelings of despair in us. 'You'll never get better,' or: 'You'll never cope with your feelings of fear. You'll always feel depressed, guilty, burdened. You'll never fight this or that temptation. You're hooked. You're an addict. Give up,' says the devil. 'Curse God and die.' But of course the devil is a liar. If we put ourselves and our trouble in the healing hand of God, if we rest and relax in his presence, if we trust his love and his wisdom, we shall find that God's healing power can and will infiltrate the situation, transforming it. There were dire predictions about the church warden whose story I told in chapter five. But they came to nothing. In chapter ten, Greg could see no way out of his depression. 'You can't help me. Nobody can,' he said. But Christ could and did. Even if a condition ends in death – and it will for all of us sooner or later – the experience of death can be transformed by the healing triumphant power of the risen Christ, as it was in the case of Greta in chapter twelve. So beware of the rigidity of hopelessness.

The second type of rigidity is perhaps more subtle. It places preconditions on the form which healing is to take. We saw in chapter five that in insomnia the more rigidly one concentrates on going to sleep, the more wakeful one is liable to become. Similarly after an operation or after a dose of flu it is never a good thing to set oneself a rigid time-table for recovery. 'On day one I shall feel in such a fashion and do this. On day two I shall feel a degree better and do that,' and so on. It rarely works that way. There are good days and bad days. Rigidity of expectation can be a barrier to recovery. Turning this sort of rigidity into the form of a prayer barely disguises it. Christian healing means letting God have his way with us, not superimposing our will upon him!

One reason why it is wrong to be rigid is that God knows the nature of the blocks to healing which have to be circumvented whereas we may not. Another reason is that we may not know where our own deepest need for healing lies. We may be conscious of a physical condition but unaware that there is a more serious spiritual condition underlying it. God's concern is with the whole of us, not just with partial or symptomatic conditions.

A man phoned me to ask if I could make his bad back better. I explained that what I had to offer him was the fullness of the healing power of Jesus Christ and that Jesus was interested not just in his back but in the whole of him, body and soul, every part of his life. There was a pause and then he said, 'That wasn't what I had in mind,' and rang off. At any rate he saw the distinction and had a glimpse of what the Church has to offer, even if he went on to reject it.

So if we wish to open ourselves to Christian healing the first step is to admit our need for healing and the second is to make ourselves available and flexible to the healing power of the Holy Spirit. We have to be prepared to pray, 'Holy Spirit, come into me and have your healing way. Help me to see the things which you wish to show me. Help me to hear the things which you wish to tell me. Help me to receive the things which you wish to give me.' If we pray in this way either for ourselves or for someone else, we must be prepared for the unexpected to happen. I think of an accountant who attended a group to pray for the health of a sick friend and unmistakably received a call to the ministry whilst doing so. I think of the many occasions when God had used one of my own prayers for healing to show me an aspect of myself which I would have preferred not to see, some facet of myself needing the healing touch of Christ.

We should not worry if the first symptoms of Christian healing appear contra-productive. A continuing openness will often reveal a reason for it. Geraldine came to see me in a greatly upset state after receiving a laying on of hands. She had undergone an experience of severe panic shortly after

the service and had to be put to bed trembling. It emerged
that she had brought a phobic condition to the service in the
hope that it would be healed. Following the service the lost
roots of her phobia had come back to consciousness. I was
able to minister to them and to her in the name of Christ. She
went on to begin to experience a new liberty.

New liberty is a characteristic of healed life in Christ. Jesus
said, 'If you rest in my word . . . you shall know the truth and
the truth shall make you free . . . and if the Son makes you
free, then your freedom will be real and true.' (John, chapter
8, verses 31, 32 and 36). 'Where the spirit of the Lord is,
there,' says St Paul, 'is liberty' (2 Corinthians 3: 17).

A final thought about our own healing, our own liberation.
Christian healing is not just a flash in the pan, a magic
moment; it is a way of life, a life-long process. Who needs
healing? I do. And I shall do tomorrow, and the day after,
and the day after that. The complexities of healing match the
complexities of my own body, mind and spirit, the complexities of my thoughts and words and deeds, the complexities of every relationship in my past, present and future. And
it is never a static or self-restricted influence. When I receive
freely, I am expected to give freely. Just as we are loved in
order to love, and forgiven in order to forgive, so *we are
healed in order to heal.*

CHAPTER SIXTEEN

Where do we go from here?

If I have a vision for tomorrow's Church, it is that it will receive God's healing power more deeply and channel it into the world more effectively. By the Church I do not mean just 'them' – the powers that be, the leaders in high places. Nor do I mean just 'them' – the folk with magic in their hands because they have perhaps some special psychic gift for healing. I mean 'us' – ordinary folk like me, and perhaps like you.

I hope that the picture I have conveyed of St George's, Hyde, is that of an ordinary church, a church with which anyone can easily identify. St Paul speaks of 'gifts of healing' in 1 Corinthians, chapter 12. Anyone having such a gift must praise God for it and use it in God's service. But if you do not feel that you have such a gift, take comfort. At St George's our basic awareness has not so much been that of having any sort of special gift, but rather that of having a specific command from Christ. One of our Church officers feels he may have a gift of healing, but there is no evidence that healing takes place to a greater extent when he is involved in our laying on of hands service than when he is not. Similarly when we had our Mission of Teaching and Healing most of the instances in which healing and blessing were reported involved a laying on of hands not by George Bennett but by the other clergy who assisted. Christ's command to the Church is, 'Heal'. If we obey him, we may leave the provision of 'gifts' in his hands.

In an attempt to obey Christ's command to heal we have instituted a ministry with healing as its aim both inside and outside the services of the church. Many other churches and groups have done the same thing. In the appendix to this book I have investigated four of them and reported on my findings. There is considerable variety in the forms which the ministry of healing can take. Sometimes it can appear sensational, extraordinary, even bizarre. By contrast our ministry

71

has been a quiet, unemotional and in many ways rather ordinary affair. Initially there was no publicity because we did not want it and because there really was not much to publicise. There was no outright hostility to this ministry in the church, perhaps because many of our congregation were not convinced that anything important was happening. Some still feel that way, although the consciousness of the centrality of Christian healing in the life and ministry of the Church is steadily increasing. In one way I regret that I cannot write a more spectacular book, but in another way perhaps it is good that it should be so. Our very ordinariness is your comfort and your challenge. This book is a manual by a beginner for beginners. If Christian healing can come to St George's, Hyde, it can come anywhere!

Whilst I have been writing this book my diocesan Bishop has asked me to move on to another parish and I have said that I will do so. By the time you read it I expect I shall be there. It has been said to me, 'How can you think of leaving? What about your ministry of healing?' The answer is that the ministry is not mine or St George's, it is Christ's. He can continue it at St George's, Hyde. He can develop it in my new parish. It does not depend on any individual set of hands or any individual locality. It does not depend on any particular style of ministry or level of churchmanship. It depends on Christ's command, his wisdom, faithfulness and power.

So where do we go from here? I have tried to make this a practical book, so may I add a further practical suggestion? May I suggest that you collect a small group of fellow Christians and together go through the chapters of this book critically and in detail one by one. Ask of each chapter the question, '*Is this true?*' You may care to apply five tests of the truth. 1. Is each chapter true to the teaching of the Bible *as a whole*, so far as you understand it? 2. Is it true to what you know of Christ? 3. Is it true to reason? – for God gave us minds and he means us to use them. 4. Is it true to experience, both personal experience and the experience of history, including the traditional experience of the Church? 5. Is it true to the promptings of the Holy Spirit in you? These are five tests which I regularly apply to new ideas and propositions. If an idea is false it founders on one or more of these tests, sometimes on all of them.

As far as the illustrative incidents and the case histories are concerned, the names are fictitious and one or two details have been changed, but basically they are true and as objective as I have been able to make them. Where possible I have avoided technical medical or psychiatric terminology, because it would seem wrong for me to set myself up as an amateur doctor or psychiatrist, although our spheres of concern overlap to some extent. I have also been on my guard against overstatement and wishful thinking. These stories can of course be paralleled and exceeded by stories in many other books about Christian healing. See for instance the two books by George Bennett, which were mentioned in chapter four.

If, after critical scrutiny, your group comes to the conclusion that this book is basically true, may I then suggest a second question: *'Is it important?'* Not all truth is equally important. The truth, for instance, about the mating habits of a wart-hog might only be important to a zoologist or another wart-hog! It would have a limited concern. Is Christian healing like that – interesting only to those who like that sort of thing? Or is it, as I have been suggesting, universal in its application and importance? Here are some questions to help you decide. Do you believe Christ really did heal folk who were ill in body, mind and spirit? Do you believe him when he says, 'Where two or three are gathered together in my name, I am there in the midst?' Do you believe that Jesus has not changed – that he is the same yesterday, today and tomorrow? Then it follows that the Christ in the midst of Christians is a healing Christ today as ever and that he still bids the Church to be healed in order to heal. Is that important? Does every single chapter in this book, however inadequate and partial, point to something central and urgent in God's call to the Church?

The third question follows naturally. If there is both truth and importance in the concept of Christian healing, then *what are we going to do about it?* It was a question I had to face for myself and still have to face. The effectiveness of today's Church and tomorrow's Church depends to a large extent on our answer to that question. Is the Church prepared, are we prepared to be available to the healing power of Christ? Will we admit our need, our sickness? Will we admit his power? Will we hear his call to channel his healing into this sick world at every level?

'Faithful is he who calls.' How faithful are we?

APPENDIX 1

Carrie Oates and the ministry of Healing in Cornwall

Miss Carrie Oates is one of the most unforgettable people I have ever met. As I write about her in the summer of 1975 her age is eighty-four-and-a-half years, but you would never guess it from her spritely body, her lively mind, her over-flowing spirit. You would never guess it from the twinkle in her eye or the length of her working day or the vigour which characterises the whole of her life – particularly her ministry of healing. She rises at six-thirty each morning, says her prayers, prepares her breakfast, opens the day's letters (about forty of them every week), prays around them, answers them in her own hand. The phone rings. The door bell rings. Sometimes she has to travel to some other part of Cornwall, speaking, leading prayers, laying on hands. Or she has one of her regular meetings for healing prayer to conduct in Truro. Or someone comes for a personal interview.

I was fortunate to find her free on a sunny Saturday after-noon in July 1975. For five hours we sat in the front room of her Truro home whilst she told me the story of her pioneer work in the ministry of healing in Cornwall. It felt like five minutes! As we talked, my tape recorder was switched on. So later in this chapter I can quote a selection of the things she said exactly.

She told me first about her own healing, because it was an experience of being healed which launched her into the ministry of healing. Back in 1938 Carrie Oates developed the eye disease glaucoma. She became unable to bear light. For sixteen years she lived mostly in a darkened room with a green blind permanently covering the window. If she went out she had to wear dark green goggles with leather sides and even so daylight was painful to her. However in 1954 she received a remarkable instantaneous healing. A friend per-suaded her to attend a service of healing in a Congregational

74

Church in Brighton. It was conducted by Brother Mandus, now widely known as the founder of the Blackpool-based World Healing Crusade, though then still in the early days of his ministry. She told me how in that Brighton church, in an atmosphere of intensely expectant congregational prayer, Brother Mandus asked her to take off her goggles and put his hands over her eyes. There followed an experience of intense heat ('Terrific, like nothing I had ever felt before') and then as the hands were taken away, she found herself able to look around the church, even at the lights on the ceiling which had been torture to her only moments before. The pain was gone and 'the light was good'.

Carrie Oates never wore her goggles from that time onwards. Now she walks out in the bright Cornish sunshine and does not even have a pair of sunglasses. Her friends were astonished to see her walking about without her goggles, looking better than she had looked for years and again and again she was asked how it happened. As she repeated the story, the conviction grew in her that she was called to bring the ministry of healing to Truro. Her first thought was to organise a service of healing conducted by Brother Mandus. This she did in the Women's Institute in 1957. It was not possible to use a church. There was an Anglican bann at the time in the diocese on public services of healing in churches and no suitable Free Church was available. But even though there was some degree of clerical suspicion, the service was attended by three hundred people and Miss Oates glowed as she recollected, 'God saw that, though I couldn't get a church, two of the most wonderful healings came to a Congregational minister with eye-trouble and to an old Anglican clergyman seriously ill in hospital.'

A second service was conducted in the Women's Institute at Truro by Brother Mandus in 1960. Miss Oates told me of a baby brought to this service, paralysed in one leg and arm. Brother Mandus took the babe in his arms and prayed – and the paralysed leg kicked out! A third service was held in 1963. This time permission was given for it to be held in Miss Oates's parish church, St John's, Truro. St John's church has been available for subsequent services also.

One factor which was influential in changing the diocesan policy was that from 1957 onwards Carrie Oates organised a regular meeting twice a month for healing prayer. Many were helped and influenced by these meetings, including some who were later to offer themselves for the ministry (Miss Oates calls them 'my boys'). At first the meetings were held in the Women's Institute. Later a large front room in a friend's private flat was put at the group's disposal and since then meetings have been held every Tuesday evening and once a month on a Wednesday afternoon.

Carrie Oates was invited here and there to speak about her experiences and the ministry of healing began to spread as she and her 'boys' and others who had a concern for Christian healing made their convictions increasingly felt throughout Cornwall. One of her 'boys', a layman, Stanley Thomas, has been licensed by the Bishop as a diocesan healer and exercises a remarkable ministry in his home at Marazion and elsewhere.

A Christian Centre which has the promotion of Christian healing as a major aim has been founded in a lovely old house called 'Trelowarren' at Mawgan-in-Meneage, near Helston, the home of John and Jonet Vyvyan. The Vyvyans have put part of it including a fifteenth century chapel at the disposal of those who have come to be known as the 'Trelowarren Fellowship'. Much of the initial inspiration for this came from the Rev'd Kingsley Halden, a Methodist minister from Jamaica, whose personal concern with Christian healing had already led him to have his church at Illogan, near Redruth, dedicated to the ministry of healing and to institute a quarterly ecumenical service of healing there. The Rector of Mawgan, the Rev'd Beverley Thompson (one of Miss Oates's 'boys') became the chaplain of the Fellowship. Carrie Oates herself became its Honorary President. The Fellowship was started in 1974. The chapel was restored and dedicated in January 1975 at an ecumenical service led jointly by the Bishop of Truro, the Chairman of the Methodist District and the Roman Catholic Dean of Cornwall. The centre is now in regular use.

I was also told of the ministries of healing at Penzance, St Austell, Budock (Falmouth), Grampound, St Buryan and elsewhere.

Carrie Oates added the practice of the laying on of hands to her ministry of healing in 1973 at the age of eighty-two. When asked to do so she ministers this either privately in the front room of her home or publicly at services of Christian healing. However she regards as her principal gift – now well tried and abundantly exercised – the ability to lead people into the silence of healing prayer. Let her speak for herself. You may find, as I do, that as you read her words you are yourself led into a healing stillness.

'My gift,' she says, 'is to draw people into the stillness of God's presence; to help them realise the presence of God and then to talk to them about the life of God within. To live in the absolute awareness of the presence of God, that is the goal of earth's life.

'The highest form of healing is the absolute awareness of the fact that "in Him we live and move and have our being", that the life of God is in the billions of cells that make up the human body. Each one of them holds potentially the life of God. We have potentially the same power that our Lord had and so fully recognised. He couldn't have made it plainer. "The Kingdom of God is within you." The place where God dwells is within you. He prayed, "That they may be one, Father, even as Thou and I are one, I in them and thou in me, that they may be one." We are "heirs of God and joint heirs with Christ". It is the awareness of all this that will bring healing. When we can drop our fixations on our symptoms and the names of our troubles and instead say to ourselves, "The life of God is here", if we can come into the stillness, into the awareness of his presence and hold that thought – you can get up without a pain, if you've sat down with one!

'If you've got a harmony in your mind, it's the mind that is in charge of all the cells in the body. What you think in your mind is translated into the action of the cells. If you've got discord in your mind, then your cells are out of the divine order, but if you've got rhythm, if you've got harmony in your mind, and you keep your mind happy in the love of God, then those cells are aware of that and they come into a divine order, into a divine rhythm. And divine rhythm is healing.

'I feel that the highest form of prayer is contained in the words "Be still and know God". At our meeting for healing prayer we come into the stillness of the awareness of God's presence. Then at the moment of deepest stillness, I lift the book with the names of the many who have asked us for healing prayer, and I hold it lifted, and we give thanks that God is using us as channels through our love and faith for his power to go out to them. Then afterwards when I feel it right, I lower the book and make the general prayers aloud. We pray for all people who are sick in hospitals and nursing homes or in their own homes and we pray for surgeons, doctors and nurses. And then we sent out our love to the millions of hungry and homeless, the frightened, the bereaved, the victims of violence. We are just aware of the Presence, and we send out love, realising that the life of God is in every soul on earth, just as it's in us.'

Many have derived benefit from Carrie Oates's gift of leading others into the silence of healing prayer. 'God,' she says, 'has given me the ability to draw people together.' Of those drawn together a number have gone out afterwards not only with an experience of God's healing power for the whole man but with a desire to communicate it to others. It is to a large extent thanks to Carrie Oates that Cornwall is now better endowed with the ministry of healing than many other areas.

Let Miss Oates have the last word — in fact several last words. She is so eminently quotable that I cannot resist passing this little anthology of her sayings on to you.

About healing the whole man. 'Divine healing is not just a service with a laying on of hands. It's a way of life, a way of love, a way of faith.'

About laying on of hands. 'Your only job in laying on hands is to be aware of the Father.'

About preaching. 'When you get up into the pulpit to preach, love all your people, even the awkward ones. Love the Christ in them, which may not be manifesting in them at the moment but it's your job to bring out.'

About suffering. 'I find it very easy to speak because I am speaking mainly from experience, and when it's anything to do with healing, if you've suffered it gives you an understanding. It gives you something which makes your suffering worthwhile in enabling you to help somebody else.'

About tiredness. 'When you're tired, sit down quietly for a few minutes and think of the presence of God, because he's everywhere. Close your eyes. Think quietly of the words, "made in the image of God" and, "the life of God in every cell". And there's no weariness in God. There's no time limit to his strength. You'll begin to cheer up.'

About effective witness. 'Your effect on other people is tremendous if you can radiate the life and the light of God.'

About dealing with trouble. 'I always think of the words of a Scots woman, a Baptist, who said that the way to deal with trouble was to "Give it to the Lord and then mind your own business!" '

About spiritual warfare. 'We're all being attacked today. Every person on the spiritual path is being attacked today. The powers of evil are seeking to overcome the strongholds of light – but the strongholds of light will win.'

About old age. 'There is no age in spirit, is there? We live by the spirit of God and the number of years don't matter unless you fix your mind on the number of years and think it's about time I looked a bit older.'

Carrie Oates's favourite prayer. 'Thank you, Father.'

Finally, her personal goal. 'To live in the absolute awareness of the presence of God, that is the goal of earth's life. That is what I pray I may fully realise before God calls me.'

As the five-hour interview drew to a close Miss Oates said sympathetically, 'You look tired,' and I realised that I was. But I had to admit that she looked as fresh as a daisy!

APPENDIX 2

The Healing Ministry
in a Derbyshire Parish Church

'Dear Mr Griffith – I do feel that you would like to know that while you were praying with me my migraine disappeared and I was completely free from the nausea I had had for many hours. Thank you. May God continue to bless your work of healing.' So ran a letter received by the Rev'd Geoffrey Griffith not long before I talked with him in August 1975 at his vicarage at Chapel-en-le-Frith, Derbyshire. It is a small example of an element of his ministry which he has regarded as centrally important ever since he was a curate.

He told me how he first became involved in the ministry of healing when in 1951, as a curate, he came across a man in church weeping bitterly because his wife was desperately ill in hospital and the doctors had said they could do no more for her. They went together to the hospital and found her in a coma. No communication with her seemed possible, so Geoffrey Griffith prayed and anointed her. This happened on a Saturday. He visited the hospital again on the following Monday and was startled to find her up and about the ward. Her recovery was so rapid that when he paid a third visit on Wednesday he found she had been discharged!

She told him subsequently that whilst she was in the coma it felt as though there was some dark presence at the foot of her bed, a presence which threatened to envelop her, but suddenly it vanished and she was surrounded by light. From that moment she knew that all was going to be well.

Since then both during the remainder of his curacy and in the two parishes in which he has served as incumbent (Waddington, near Lincoln, and his present parish of Chapel-en-le-Frith) he has regarded the ministry to the sick by laying on of hands, anointing and prayer as an integral part of his work. Often he has found himself able to communicate peace, rest and joy. Sometimes physical healing has followed.

He told me, for instance, of Marianne, given up as dying after a cerebral haemorrhage. Week by week she received a laying on of hands until she made a complete recovery. Then there was eighty-year-old Sarah who collapsed with a severe jaundice condition and was taken into hospital for intensive care. She too recovered completely with the aid of prayer and the laying on of hands.

Melanie was emotionally disturbed and subject to severe migraines. After prayer and the laying on of hands her migraines ceased, her attitude to life was healed. She was able to come off all the drugs which had been prescribed for her. Norah suffered two heart attacks and her life was in doubt, but she made a sound recovery after receiving prayer and a laying on of hands.

Ellen needed more than this. She was a chronic rheumatoid arthritic and worse than her physical condition was the fear which dogged her – fear of dying, fear of being sent away from home, fear of being overwhelmed by the power of evil. A simple form of exorcism was needed here (though without actually using the word exorcism). Exorcism, Holy Communion, and the regular and frequent laying on of hands eventually led to a lessening of the arthritic condition and a complete release from fear.

Geoffrey Griffith does not regard himself as having a special gift of healing. He regards healing as a central ingredient in the life of the Church as a whole and feels there is no reason why every local church should not share in it. One element of prime importance for him has been that in both his parishes he has been supported by a healing-prayer group, largely consisting of people with a personal experience of healing, who therefore feel a call to meet once a fortnight to channel God's healing power to others and to undergird the ministry of their Vicar. Even with their help physical healing is not automatic. Almost invariably there is new peace, rest and joy but sometimes the physical condition may seem untouched. I asked him why he felt this should be so. He said that there were many reasons. Sometimes people do not really want to be healed, perhaps because they feel the need of the attention and care which sickness can attract. Sometimes there is an attitude of non-faith or negative thinking on the part of relatives which acts as a block to recovery. Often the Church is insufficiently whole-hearted in its commitment to the ministry of healing, and so the power to heal is weakened.

Geoffrey Griffith longs for the whole of his congregation to achieve the same commitment to Christian healing which is evident in his prayer group. With a view to encouraging this he arranged a George Bennett mission of teaching and healing in July 1974. As he is Rural Dean of Buxton as well as Vicar of Chapel-en-le-Frith he was able to involve other churches in the Deanery. As at St George's, Hyde, so at Chapel-en-le-Frith the mission was a great event, culminating in a service of Christian healing attended by about four hundred.

Subsequently there have been signs of the emergence of a new climate in the church as a whole. Regular services of healing are being held on Sunday afternoons once every two months. The prayer group has increased in size. Geoffrey Griffith and his fellow-workers in the healing ministry face the future with interest and expectation.

APPENDIX 3

The Healing Ministry
in a Cheshire Charismatic Group

The Rev'd Bill Davies, Methodist Minister and Senior Lecturer in Religious Studies at Padgate College, Warrington, became involved in the Charismatic movement in 1970, and as a consequence he and his wife Barbara felt moved to open their home in Thelwall, Cheshire (an area well known to me because I was Vicar there from 1962 to 1968), as a place where others with a similar involvement could meet, study, pray and have fellowship.

Every Tuesday evening the house was opened and people came from near and far. Their home is a fairly small house with a proportionately small front room. Sometimes the room and the hall outside were full and people sat on the stairs. However the problem of lack of space proved to be a means of growth. People who came from a distance started their own groups, and there are now similar fellowships at Knutsford, Chester, Winsford, Orrell (near Wigan), Whiston (near Prescott), Blackpool, Birkenhead, Swinton (Manchester) and elsewhere. Also the Vicar of Thelwall offered the use of the vicarage to the group on the second Tuesday of the month and the Parish Church on the last Tuesday of the month.

At first the meetings consisted of prayer and praise and Bible study of a personal kind. Each member asked, 'What does this passage say to me? How does it affect my life?' After about twelve months a visitor from Somerset spoke in tongues and there was an interpretation and from then on the members felt it increasingly right that the exercise of charismatic gifts should also have their place at group meetings – tongues, the interpretation of tongues, singing in the Spirit, prophecies, and visions recounted and interpreted. Within this context the ministry of healing has come to have a place of central importance. Sometimes a 'word of knowledge' reveals that a member of the group is in need of healing, or there is a personal request for healing, and those members who feel led to do so lay on hands or, if it is felt right, there is an anointing.

Bill Davies told me of various instances of healing. A man with a bad heart attended one of the meetings in church. Hands were laid on him for healing and a prophecy was given that God was going to give him more work to do in the future than in the past. His symptoms disappeared and in fact he was able to increase his work load, and at a subsequent meeting he returned to testify to both these facts. Another man came to the group with a severe earache which had troubled him for a long time. The group prayed with him and instantaneously the earache cleared and has not returned.

On one occasion members of the group travelled some distance to a man in terrible pain from a virulent cancer. They laid hands on him and prayed for his wholeness. He died two or three weeks later but was free from pain from the moment of laying on of hands. A strange additional feature here was that at the moment of laying hands on the sufferer, his sister in another room unexpectedly and for the first time began to speak in tongues.

Another man came to the group having lost his voice. He could not speak and the group prayed that God would restore his voice. Next day he telephoned and his voice was clear as a bell.

A professional woman who was having a nervous breakdown made contact with the group. She was on the phone to the Davieses every day. They and the group stayed with her in her trouble. She said she hated the group and its meetings, but she kept coming. Eventually after two years she came through the worst of her mental trouble. She also regained a lost faith. The healing was gradual and she had to go right into the abyss – but the group went with her.

Another of the incidents reported took place after a Sunday evening service at a local Methodist church at which Bill Davies had been preaching. After the service a youth was found still in his seat, weeping. He was invited into the vestry and there it emerged that he felt himself possessed by evil. He said he heard voices which told him to do evil things. He had had a chequered life, much of which had been spent either at an approved school or on probation. Bill Davies told me that though his first reaction was to send the lad to a doctor or psychiatrist, after they had talked for an hour, he found himself rather to his surprise saying, 'Come into church. If you believe you are possessed by evil, Jesus can deal with that.' They went back into church and after a prayer of penitence, asking for God's cleansing and forgiveness, Bill Davies three times commanded whatever it was which carried the affliction to be bound and to be cast out in the name of Jesus. After the first time the lad said that the voices were quieter, after the second time he said they were calling, 'Jesus, Jesus, Jesus,' and there was a ringing in his ears. After the third time, he said, 'It's gone! Whatever it is has gone!' Then with a little encouragement he prayed that the Spirit of Jesus would come and fill his life so that the spirit of evil could not gain access again. Since then he has been free from the voices, and has changed in various ways, cleaning himself up, getting himself a job, establishing a right relationship with his parents again, and attending the Tuesday Fellowship until his job required him to work on a Tuesday evening.

This was a case of obeying an impulsion, of being moved to do something and therefore doing it. This is a characteristic of the group's healing ministry. The group does not so much believe it has a gift of healing, but rather that there are gifts of healing available to Christians, a new and individual gift for every new situation, each depending on a fresh anointing by the Spirit. It does not matter who administers healing within the group, so long as he or she or they are truly moved to do it, though in practice there are about eight of the group who do it more than others.

Bill Davies freely admitted that there were instances of apparent failure in healing – for instance a woman in a coma who was prayed for but did not recover and a spastic lad much prayed for but apparently little better. I asked him why he thought it was that Christian healing sometimes seems to work at a physical level and why sometimes not. He replied with honesty that he just does not know the answer. Personal honesty is a characteristic of Bill Davies's life and thought. I knew this from my previous years as Vicar of Thelwall. So banking on this I asked him, rather presumptuously, a series of awkward questions about charismatic groups and Christian healing.

There are hundreds of charismatic groups around the country, similar in many ways to the group in Thelwall. I asked Bill Davies whether he thought that members of charismatic groups could be thought to have achieved a greater measure of wholeness than an average cross-section of the population. Did they display greater health of body, mind and spirit than others, I asked. Or does there seem nothing to choose between them and others? Or do they actually seem less healthy? He paused. 'Now, that's a question that needs some thought,' he said. 'We attract a number of people who come to us with needs, because they can't go anywhere else, and therefore you do have a number of neurotic people involved in the movement. But they come because they will be listened to here, they will be cared for, and they will receive some form of ministry and help. And for that matter, the sick and the neurotic went to Jesus. So I would not say that charismatics are healthier than others, but I would say that most people in our groups are on the way to wholeness.'

My next question was equally difficult. Neurosis is a great counterfeiter. A neurotic personality is capable of reproducing charismatic phenomena without an underlying experience of the Spirit. Worse still – the devil is a liar and can counterfeit the externals of the gifts of the spirit with frightening accuracy – even sometimes producing the semblance of healing. So my question was, 'How do you know that the experiences of your group are the genuine product of the Holy Spirit and not a counterfeit? What sort of tests do you apply?' The answer was, 'There have been times when things have gone wrong and it has been known – perhaps because of the quality of the discussion or because of the atmosphere. We do not accept a gift as valid unless it comes through someone who has confessed Jesus as Lord. The quality of witness is one test of the spirit. Also: "Though I speak with the tongues of men and of angels and have not love I am a sounding brass and a tinkling cymbal." So the test of wholeness has to be backed up by the test of love. Also a true spiritual gift builds up the body of Christ. This is another test. Anything that causes division we would not recognise as a true spiritual gift. The consensus of the gossip provides another test. The body tests the spirit of the prophets. It can happen also that an individual with discernment of spirits will on occasion offer a rebuke.'

'But suppose,' I asked, 'that the whole group goes wrong? How do you guard against wishful thinking and self decep-

tion as a group?' 'The test,' he answered, 'is in the out-
workings of the group in the world. "By their fruits you shall
know them." The degree of group-realism is another test. So
is the ecumenical effectiveness of the group. We are by no
means perfect. We are a body being fashioned. There are
occasional personality clashes. We recognise them for what
they are. We think that the devil tries to use them. We think
and talk and pray them through. Honesty is essential. If a
group is "glory, glory" all the way and nobody is honest, it
can get artificial and insincere. I think our own group can
stand the test of honesty, but I think we need to apply it
more often and more rigorously. There is much that is wrong
with the charismatic movement. We have exaggeration. We
have wishful thinking. We have unfortunate claims that are
made. But when you have said all this, there is something
there which is very real and very much of God.'

My next question was, 'Do you get the sense that people in
your group have grown in stature over the years and that they
are more "whole" than they were when they started?' – a
question which points right to the heart of the presence or
absence of Christian healing. The answer was, 'Yes, some of
them. We have a long way to go, all of us. But the group has
shown us things which were wrong with us which we did not
know. The fact of the group interacting in the Spirit, a sort of
Holy Spirit group-dynamic, has shown us needs. Sometimes
we have had a confession – perhaps selfishness, lack of trust,
or resentment against another person. I would like to see it
happen more often.'

Finally came my most personal question. 'In what sense,
Bill, have you been aware of yourself being made more whole
over the years by being involved in all this?' And the answer:
'Initially I had twelve months of uninterrupted riding on
cloud nine. Then I was hit by a vocational crisis which
knocked me for six. Afterwards I regained balance again. All
of this has made me realise that I am dispensable. It has made
me realise that it is not so much what *I* do but what *God* does
that counts. It has given me a greater faith than I had
hitherto. It has made me more open towards other people. It
has also made me aware that I have a lot of needs and sins
to be dealt with. I have realised that it is not "glory, glory"
all the way. When people talk about "having the victory"
what they sometimes forget, and what I have sometimes forgotten, is that a victory presupposes that there is a battle to

be fought. It has also made me realise that there is so much further to go.'

It was, I thought, a good answer; the answer of a man who, though he knows he has much further to go, is certainly on the way; the answer of a man accepting and channelling Christian healing into the world.

Let Bill Davies have the last word. 'What is most important is not seeking after experiences of gifts, or experiences of miracles or powers. Let them follow if they will. The important thing is the fullness of the Spirit of Christ himself within the life of the believer.'

APPENDIX 4

Gifts in Somerset

Few of the people whom we have so far considered would claim to have a gift for healing. They are aware of Christ's command to heal. They feel impelled to seek to obey it. The provision of gifts they leave in the hands of the Lord. But there are those for whom involvement in Christian healing happens the other way round. Their primary awareness is of personally having some sort of gift of healing, and for them Christian healing means offering this already-existing gift to our Lord.

It was in search of such gifts that in December 1975 I drove down the M6 and the M5 to Somerset to visit the little village of Moorlinch, near Bridgwater, where the Vicar, the Rev'd Francis Vere Hodge, had reported to me that he was working closely with two ladies who were endowed with gifts of healing and who seemed to be infecting others with similar gifts.

A parish pamphlet which he sent me described the situation like this. 'We say of many that they have a gift, perhaps for music, languages, medicine or technology, or perhaps for simply living but there are also a number of people who have the gift, to a lesser or greater extent, of healing. Here in the vicinity of Moorlinch there are several of us who have been shown by God that he wishes to channel his healing power through us, either to supplement medical healing or to help in cases where, at present, medicine is unable to help. Although we are practising Christians, our services are of course available to anyone of any religion or of no religion at all. We find that we are also able to help animals.

'The healing power, which seems to behave in some ways like electricity, usually flows down the arms of the person who is transmitting it, and out to the person receiving it. Most people can feel the power as warmth, coldness, or a tingling vibration, and this is indicative that the healing power is

89

working in them. A few people feel nothing at all, but still benefit.

'Healing is given (a) at monthly healing services in church, usually at Moorlinch on a Tuesday evening, (b) at a private house, "Forsters" in Shapwick. The two full-time workers are Miss Valery P. White and Miss Rosemary K. V. Cave.'

I spent two days talking with Miss White, Miss Cave, Francis Vere Hodge, and with a number of people who claimed to have received healing from them. The story which I heard in bits and pieces can perhaps best be repeated as a chronological sequence.

In 1965 Rosemary Cave was sitting typing at a desk in London. She was working as a secretary. Suddenly she was caught up into a strange 'out of the body' experience, an experience of what she calls cosmic consciousness. She told me how she 'was taken up and up to become a centre of spiritual power, one with the origin of life, one with the power which creates and re-creates'. And then she was back at her desk, at her typewriter. She found herself praying, 'God, if I am to use this power please let me use it for good.'

Later she went back home, still in something of a daze. Her mother was in bed with rheumatism. She rearranged her mother's bedclothes and her mother said that she thought something was wrong with her electric blanket as she could feel electricity. Rosemary turned off the blanket. Still her mother said she could feel electricity. Then they found it was coming from Rosemary's hands. They also found it was taking away her mother's rheumatic pain. Rosemary had been given, it seemed, a healing gift, and during the months which followed she used it as opportunity arose.

In 1966, her friend, Valery White, also received a healing gift. They had talked about Rosemary's gift and Valery, coming from a medical family, had been greatly interested. One Friday evening they were together and Rosemary complained of ear trouble. Valery touched her friend's ears and suddenly it felt, in her own words, as though her 'arms were hollow and hot water was pouring through'. She knew that she too had received a gift of healing and next day she went into church and dedicated her hands to the service of God at the altar. I asked her if she felt it was a specifically Christian gift and she answered that she felt it might come to a follower of any religion, but that she had never come across an atheist with such a gift.

She then began, like Rosemary, to minister healing as occasion arose. She used several memorable phrases as she described her ministry. 'The power leaps in your hands,' she said. 'It feels rather like nettles yesterday.' She had no doubt about the gift's objective reality. Sometimes, she said, it stops her watch, and so she now always takes her watch off before ministering healing.

In 1967 Valery White met the Rev'd Francis Vere Hodge. He had long had a concern about Christian healing and had laid hands on the sick in obedience to Christ's command. He invited Miss White to help him in his parish and in particular to minister healing at a regular service of healing in Moorlinch church. The services began in February 1968. Rosemary Cave often travelled from London so that she too could have a part in them.

In 1969 Valery White moved into 'Forsters', a lovely thatched cottage at Shapwick (a village not far from Moorlinch) and began to exercise a ministry of healing from there.

In 1970 Rosemary gave up her London job and moved into the vicinity of Moorlinch so that she too could exercise a full-time ministry of healing.

They started an appointments system at 'Forsters', spacing appointments at hourly intervals. Their practice when laying on hands was to take some little time over it – six or seven minutes for each individual at church services (so that only a dozen or so receive the laying on of hands at each service) and up to thirty minutes at a private appointment. The Vicar played his part too both privately and at the healing services, anointing the sick and joining in the laying on of hands. Soon he too found himself developing a gift of healing.

Various healings were reported to me. I was told of three multiple sclerosis patients who now show a marked improvement. I heard of a cure of asthma. I heard of a woman with gall stones who received a laying on of hands. Afterwards no gall stones could be found and a projected operation was cancelled. I was told of skin conditions which had cleared. 'Headaches,' I was told, 'invariably clear. You can almost whisk them away with your hands.'

On the other hand, some people have not been healed. At the healing service which I attended some of those present were clearly far from whole in spite of regular reception of the laying on of hands. One of those present made a point of telling me that her trouble seemed not to be helped at all. Others however who had been helped and healed were introduced to me and told me their stories.

I spent some time with a psychiatric social worker who brought a friend to a service of healing and found that in the process she herself received healing. She had suffered a Potts fracture of the ankle which had only partly healed. She was unsteady on her feet and had a certain amount of pain when driving her car. Also the use of her right hand was impaired. At the service there was a spontaneous healing of her ankle and in about three weeks time her hand returned to normal. This happened in September 1974. Since then there has been no recurrence of her trouble. A year after her healing, whilst attending another service of healing, she felt a tingling in her fingertips and a longing to lay hands on others. She is now developing a gift of healing herself. She told me of instances of healing which had occurred during the exercise of her new gift – the easing of a shoulder pain, the clearing of a face rash. When I talked to her she told me that she was considering joining the Moorlinch healers on a full-time basis, living by faith without a salary, just as the others do. 'Why,' I asked her, 'do you want to heal?' She answered simply, 'Because God does not want any to be ill and because he is going to use healing gifts both to make people better and to bring people back to Christ.'

I also had a telephone conversation with a twenty-nine-year-old doctor. He came to see Valery White at 'Forsters' because he had a cancer of the adrenal gland and was very worried and distressed at the prospect of a forthcoming operation. As he received a laying on of hands the pain eased temporarily and the worry vanished completely. Valery White felt a strong conviction which she passed on to him that he would be healed and that on his recovery he would himself develop a ministry of spiritual healing. The operation was a success. A growth weighing eight and a half pounds was removed. He told me, 'I am convinced that I had to go through this to experience spiritual healing. After the laying on of hands I had no more fear. I never worried about the future again. Now I want to research into spiritual healing. I believe that man is on the verge of a new awareness of his spiritual dimension and of the immense resources and potentiality of his spirit through meditation and prayer and spiritual healing.' Please God he may be right.

Three final points.

1. In spite of the mysteries of Moorlinch (and there are more mysteries in that village than I have been able to reveal in this chapter) I am convinced that no one should wait to experience a 'gift' before embarking upon a ministry of healing. I am not even convinced that the healing power is greater when a person feels he possesses a gift than if he lays on hands simply in obedience to the command of Christ.

The Rev'd Francis Vere Hodge showed me this letter dated August 1965. 'You may remember that last September you held a healing service for our baby daughter. My wife and I thought that you would like to know that we have taken her back to the specialist who tells us that she can now no longer be considered spastic. We were originally told that she might never walk, but now at fifteen months she walks everywhere. The specialist said that he had known of only one such instance of recovery and he could give no medical reason so we feel it could well be a miracle.'

The letter, signed by the little girl's father, dates from the period *before* Francis Vere Hodge considers he received his gift of healing.

2. The prospect of a young doctor researching seriously into the spiritual element in healing is a significant and encouraging one. There cannot be too much honest, intelligent thought about this subject both inside and outside the Church, if two pitfalls are to be avoided. One pitfall is to offer people false hope – which is unforgivable. The other is to withhold true hope – which is even worse. It seems that Christ expected that we would be able to do *more* than he did (John 14: 12), but so much has been lost during the intervening centuries. So there is a serious piece of work to be done in research and rediscovery. If we who call ourselves Christians ignore it we will be shamefully neglectful and disobedient.

3. However, thank God, there are many today who neither neglect nor disobey Christ's command to heal. In compiling these appendices, investigating churches, groups and individuals who exercise a ministry of Christian healing, the problem has not been how to find them but how to select them from the many which could have been chosen. Turning over letters in my file, I have been told of ministries of healing in London, Oxfordshire, Gloucestershire, Hampshire, Lancashire, Yorkshire, Cheshire, Derbyshire, Nottinghamshire,

Surrey, Sussex, Essex, Somerset, Kent and Cornwall. I have been told of an interesting centre of healing in Norwich which co-ordinates healing work in churches all around. I was sent a copy of the centre's magazine, 'Healing Digest', which contains on the back page a list of a further twenty-four churches in the British Isles where there is a regular ministry of healing. Out of this plethora of possibilities the four areas investigated in these appendices were picked at random – though with a little help, I now think, from the Holy Spirit.

Deliberately the areas selected involved people who are at present little known. The great ones in healing are sufficiently well known already and sometimes seem far out of our reach. But when ordinary people in ordinary churches and ordinary walks of life start to communicate the touch of Christ simply because they have taken his command seriously one cannot help asking, 'Why should I not join them?'

The trickle of healing is becoming a flow. If it becomes a torrent – we may see the Kingdom of God sooner than we think!